BUSINESS WITHOUT LIMITS, LLC.

Job Search Strategies To Find A Good Job Fast

A Hiring Managers Insider Secrets!

Mark Edward Duin

6/6/2012

This book contains everything you need to get a good job fast, despite economic conditions and regardless of your background or level of education.

DEDICATION

This book is dedicated to everyone who wants a fulfilling, rewarding, good paying job, but isn't really sure how to get it!

This book is dedicated to helping you land a job quickly, anytime you want or need one.

More importantly this book is dedicated to helping YOU enjoy an amazing career doing what you are designed to be successful doing!

CONTENTS

ACKNOWLEDGEMENTS

Special thanks to Zig Ziglar who taught me how to set goals and be positive at the exact time I needed to find a job! Special thanks to Og Mandino for teaching me how to love and appreciate others and to persist until I succeed. When a positive focused person masters the process of goals, the practice of love and appreciation, and the act of persisting, they become an irresistible force!

Introduction

I remember how nervous people were. It was the crazy 1980's with unemployment around 10%. Inflation was through the roof and the economy was in the toilet. No one was hiring.

Then in October of 1987 (Black Monday) stock markets around the world crashed! The U.S. markets lost over 22% of their value. Hong Kong markets lost over 45% and New Zealand about 60%. The world economy was a mess! Tough times got tougher.

Even though I was a recovering addict and a 9th grade dropout, I somehow managed to land a job back then! Things were finally looking up. For the first time in a long time I was feeling good about myself and my life. Unfortunately, things can turn on you very quickly...

As I walked into work everything seemed surreal! It felt like a slow motion train wreck taking place and no one could do anything about it. Once inside, rumors were flying. A lot of people were being called into special offices that had been set up. Some were being walked out the door. Was this really happening? What did it mean? Then it was my turn.

I quickly learned that the company was moving out of state. The good news, I still had my job for a few more weeks. The bad news, in a few weeks I would be joining millions of Americans who were already looking for a job in a down economy.

Fear, powerlessness, hopelessness and uncertainly began to seep in. I had been working so hard to stay clean and hold a job. I wondered what was going to happen to me now. Who in the world was going to hire this ex-addict 9th grade dropout?

A Good Job In 1/4th The Time!

Amazingly I landed an even better job during that awful recession of the 1980's. Even with my horrible background, limited work experience and no college degree, I was able to get a better job in about 4 weeks. Much faster than the average qualified worker who couldn't even find a job in 21 weeks.

I had just begun learning about success principles and decided to put them to the test in my own job search. Thankfully they worked! In fact they worked really well! Exactly what did I do differently than the average job seeker? You'll find out shortly.

Today I am a hiring manager for a multimillion dollar technology business. Now I understand clearly why my job search methods have worked so well over the years. I understand why I have been successful while more qualified people have failed miserably.

In this book I openly share my knowledge as a successful job seeker and my experience as a hiring manager, so you can land a good job faster. This book will be extremely helpful to you if...

• You hate job hunting and you are ready to maximize your job search to find a job you will love!

• You've always known you were capable of having a better career but weren't sure how to make that happen.

• You want to know the best career or jobs to go after for you.

• You want to know how to find great hidden job opportunities where most job seekers aren't even looking.

• You want to be confident, well prepared, and relaxed in your interviews so you can interview just like top candidates and experts do.

• You wish you could read a hiring managers mind and knew exactly how to give them what they want most.

• You want to know how to easily win more job offers!

So what do successful job seekers do differently to help them get the job over all the other candidates? Well for starters, top job candidates seem to understand these three job search success principles…

1.   There is no failure in job searching, only feedback.

2.   Correct Thoughts and Actions = Desired Results.

3.   Incorrect Thoughts and Actions = Undesired Results.

"If you keep doing what you've been doing, you'll keep getting what you've been getting!" (Zig Ziglar)

If you're not getting the results you want in your career, in your job search, or any other area of life, it simply means that what you are doing isn't working! If you want a different (better) result you just need to start doing something that "does" work. As you follow the advice and strategies outlined in this book, you will get the results you desire!

How To Never Worry About Looking For A Job Again

A few years after I landed my first good job, it seemed strange when a startup company actually sought me out because of my expertise. It was the first time another company came after me hard like that. They wanted and needed what I had. Of course my (then) boss was going to do his best to convince me to stay. It felt pretty good to be so in demand.

After carefully weighing the pros and cons I decided to go with the startup company, and I'm so glad I did. Not only did I gain a better job, I learned a valuable lesson. And that lesson is simply this…

"When we focus on doing what we are designed to do, and we continually strive to increase our value to others, opportunities abound!"

The ultimate goal in the work world is to find work that is closely aligned with your talents, skills, abilities, and your interests! The closer you are aligned to these things (in your work) the more successful you'll be.

When you find a way to maximize your natural strengths and abilities toward doing something you love to do, you will become great at what you do. People who are great at what they do are referred to as experts! And experts usually get higher pay, better working conditions, and are in much higher demand! In good times or bad there's almost always a good job for the person who is really good at what they do.

You may or may not realize this but you are already very good at something! And you are capable of being much better than you already are!

How do I know this? Well it's like this… Even though I'm very successful now, I was a street dwelling addict in my youth, and a 9th grade dropout till I was 27 years old.

Over the years I've learned that we all have incredible potential and amazing abilities. Usually the only thing holding us back is ourselves! Our limited thinking, our limited beliefs and our lack of understanding of success principles, that's what really holds us back. But all that can be easily overcome!

Today I manage a team of highly educated (some with Masters Degrees), highly paid (many over 6 figures) engineers. Amazingly I still don't even have a college degree!

Like so many successful people I've discovered that success education is more valuable than almost any other education. As you learn the principles of success sprinkled throughout this book you'll gain everything you need to succeed in almost any situation.

The truth is you can find a great job regardless of the economy. It's all about the value you have to offer. Companies need good workers, people they can count on, people who add value. Companies don't hire someone just for the fun of it. They hire people because they need things done. They look for workers who do a great job with a great attitude, and who get along well with others.

Anyone who does great work with a great attitude, and who gets along well with others can find a job no matter what the economy is doing. When you recognize your value and can effectively communicate it to potential employers, you'll get more interviews and more job offers, guaranteed!

What You Will Gain From This Book

In this book I promise to give you everything you need to successfully find a good job. I'll show you how to identify an ideal career for you, and provide you step-by-step directions on how to get a job you can love in the quickest way possible. All you have to do is follow the directions.

Success in any venture starts in the mind! So that's exactly where we will begin your job search! More than almost anything else your mindset will influence your results. If you're ready, let's turn the page and fix you up with your own powerful Job-Winning Mindset!

CHAPTER 1 – Creating Your Job-Winning Mindset

To The Victor Goes The Job!

This was going to be interesting! As I looked across my desk at the interviewee, my internal talk began. *"Note to self... wrinkled shirt, hair looks like it hasn't been washed recently...ok don't judge, this guy could be just what we need!..."* The interview begins.

Nice to meet you Bill (not his real name)! So you're interested in our Associate Network Engineering position. Can you tell me a little about your background? Yes he could...

I learned through what Bill was saying, his body language, his voice fluctuation, eye contact, comments, and many other indicators that Bill was not really what I was looking for. A nice and interesting person, yes! But from all the indications he gave me, not the right person for this job.

Every time I interview someone I'm looking for certain things. My manager mind is turned on, tuned in, and focused on identifying the best person for the position and for our company. Surprisingly I (and many other managers) look first for attitude and character traits, then for skills.

Have you ever met a highly skilled person who was full of themselves and an absolute nightmare to work with? Imagine how much fun they are to manage!

Hiring managers like to hire people who have certain character traits. These "traits" are (in many cases) more desirable than specific job skills or job experience.

Think about this. If you apply for a job along with 300 other people and 30 of you have the job skills to do the job, what would make you more desirable to hire than the other 29? Do you know?

Let's break down the traits of people who usually win job offers…

Common Traits of Job-Offer-Winners

On outward appearance, job-offer-winners are…

- Self-confident (but not cocky)
- Knowledgeable (about their own value, their work, and their industry)
- Prepared (very prepared in every aspect of the job search game)
- Effective communicators (they effectively communicate their value)
- Good people skills (they are likable and get along well with others)
- Positive upbeat attitude (they appear positive and upbeat)

So what does this have to do with "You" getting a job? Everything! These traits enable you to win job interviews and get more job offers.

Throughout this book I will make sure you learn to effectively apply these traits as much as possible as you conduct your job search!

Below are additional traits commonly found in very successful people. These additional traits often apply to successful job-winners too.

Under the surface many job-winners also have these traits…

- Focused (they know exactly what they are going after and they prepare)
- Disciplined (they put in the time and effort required to land a job)
- Determined (they keep pushing forward till they land a job)
- Honest & sincere
- Hard-working
- Loyal
- Selfless

It's easy to see why people with these traits get hired. They typically work hard, do a great job, and cause fewer problems. They get along well with others and they are good people to work with.

Hiring managers often know it's much easier to hire for attitude and train for skill than it is to hire for skill and train for attitude.

Obviously it is very important to focus on being your best in order to get a new job!

Keep all these things in mind as we go through the techniques in this book. As you follow the steps in this book and strive to be your best, you'll begin to see just how great you really are. And so will your new employer!

Creating Your Job Winning Mindset

"Whether you believe you can do a thing or you believe you cannot, you are right." (Henry Ford)

I had just been let go from my job. Unemployment was high and no one was hiring. I was an ex addict 9th grade dropout with basically two choices. Give up and go back to the streets or figure out how to get a job despite the overwhelming odds against me.

Of all the success principles I was beginning to learn, one quote kept coming back into my mind. It was this one…

"You are what you are, you are where you are, because of what's gone into your mind. You can change what you are, you can change where you are by changing what goes into your mind!" (Zig Ziglar)

Here's the deal, every hiring manager wants to interview and hire a person with a great attitude and a positive mindset. In fact I don't know of any hiring manager who enjoys interviewing a person who is negative, has mental or emotional baggage, or a chip on their shoulder. Nor do they enjoy interviewing a person who is so reserved that it's impossible to tell what kind of attitude they do have! Hiring managers are simply more inclined to hire an upbeat, positive, generous, good natured person.

Whether you think you need to improve your mindset or not please be sure to try the following exercises! You'll be surprised at what they do for you!

When you do the following winning-mindset builders your whole outlook on life improves. You'll find that your job search efforts are greatly improved! When you practice these exercises before you go to an interview, you'll notice how much better your interviews work out! Your mindset makes a huge difference in almost every situation.

If you're ready to get your mind into job winning mode, do each of the following exercises and experience some powerful mojo!

The What's Bugging Me Now Technique

Most people who are challenged with searching for a job have at least some negative thoughts floating around in their head. Fear, doubt, anger, low self-esteem, resentment…you know that sort of thing. Even a little negative thought residue is bad for you, and believe it or not other people can sense it.

This "What's bugging me now" technique and all the other techniques in this section will totally do away with any unproductive mindset. Even if you don't think you have a problem, I suggest you go through this exercise anyway. It will boost your mindset so much that you'll automatically become more charismatic and likable. And believe me that will come in handy in your next interview.

Okay here's what you do. On a piece of paper make three columns, like in the example on the next page. In column number one you'll write down everything that's bothering you, big or small. In column number two you'll write down why it bothers you. In column number three you'll write down anything positive you can do to deal with it, or anything you can do to help you accept it if there's nothing you can do about it.

Go ahead and make this list and write out every single thing you can think of that's been bothering you (big or small). This automatically helps you get all your hidden negative thoughts and feelings out of your body, out of your mind, and out onto a piece of paper where you can see them for what they really are.

It's really just "crap thinking" that doesn't do you any good. Negative thinking and worry won't change anything no matter how hard you think about it! This exercise helps you deal with underlying thoughts and feelings in a very positive way.

Before you start this exercise take notice of how you feel inside. Just take a quick check and remember what you feel like now. Then after you do this exercise, take note of how you feel inside again. Notice what an incredible feeling of freedom and relief you have. Notice how much better you feel inside. Pretty cool stuff! Now go ahead and try it for yourself.

What's Bugging Me Now Technique Example

What's Bugging Me?	Why Does It Bother Me?	What Can I Do To Deal With This Situation In The Most Positive and Generous Way?
1. I can't believe I got let go from work! Why me! I thought I was doing a good job!!! 2. How hard is	This really makes me feel like crap. I am pissed at them for letting me go. How am I going to get a job now? How can I find something equivalent or better?	I need to let go of this. I need to realize that stuff happens to everyone. This just didn't work out for me. I can start to evaluate what I really want to do. Set goals.

	Can I compete with others for the type of job I want?	Start improving and updating my skills. Learn what I need to do to get a better job doing something I can enjoy more and be really good at…
it going to be to find a job now… 3. Who would hire me…		

The Forgive and Forget Technique

You'd be amazed how many people (people I've interviewed over the years) have a chip on their shoulder. Whenever they start talking about their previous employer, previous manager or previous people they've worked with, you can see it in their face and in their body language. They get all tensed up.

No matter how they try to pretty it up with their words, it's easy to sense they have a negative mindset towards others.

Let me ask you this… if you were a hiring manager, would you rather hire a person who is upbeat, positive, kind and generous, who genuinely likes other people, or someone you sense has some negative emotional baggage? Of course most hiring managers will hire the positive upbeat person and they will stay far away from a person they sense has negative baggage.

You want to be as upbeat as possible, so this is where the "forgive and forget technique" comes in. Here's what you do…

Grab a notepad and a pen or pencil. Write-down a list of everyone you have negative feelings towards, especially if they have to do with previous places you've worked. Next to each person's name right down why you think they did the mean or stupid things they did.

It could be that they were abused when they were young, they may be going through a divorce, they may not be blessed with a good personality or a working brain (just kidding on the last part), but write down whatever you think it is that would cause them to act in those offensive ways.

Next try to think of any time you personally have been mean, un-thinking, or have done anything stupid (look deep and be honest). This should help you see that we are all human and that we all have issues from time to time. Of course some people have more issues than others, but the point is that none of us are perfect. People typically are the way they are "for a reason".

Now try to imagine the offending person as a small child. What must've happened to that beautiful innocent little child that caused them to grow up to be such a mean butt-head? Probably something not very good right?

Finally, try to feel at least a little bit sorry for them. If you have some type of faith where you pray, then pray for them to become a better person. If not, just decide to send them love in the form of positive feelings and kind thoughts. Feel sorry for them, send them love, and make a decision right now to forgive any offense they've committed.

Don't hope for justice to be served or for them to be paid back for what they've done. You don't want to be paid back for your mistakes do you? Just decide once and for all to forgive and forget. Remember the only person your negative thoughts and feelings will harm, is you. So get rid of them (the negative thoughts and feelings that is). ☺

Now if you really want to supercharge your mindset you can do the same Forgive and Forget Technique on your own self! You can do this to forgive yourself from any and all past wrongs you've done!

We're all human and we all make mistakes! Just don't hold your past against yourself. The past is gone. You have each day going forward to strive toward being your absolute best.

Forgive yourself of the past and focus on the good things you desire to do going forward. Next time you make a mistake, forgive yourself quickly and focus on doing better as you move forward!

After you complete this exercise simply rip up the paper and throw it away. You can even bury it in the ground as a symbolic way of letting it go. Just decide to release all negative thoughts towards others and yourself.

Believe me you'll be so glad you did this exercise. You'll feel so much better and you'll take less negative energy with you everywhere you go. This exercise will ultimately help you when you interview for a job because you'll be emitting more positive generous vibrations.

Good Vibes That Help You Get Hired

Have you ever walked into a room where there was a person who was extremely upbeat, positive and energetic? Did you notice how this person's energy positively uplifted everyone around them? Now, can you remember a time when you walked into a room where there was a very negative, upset, angry person? Did you notice how the room had a very thick, dark vibration to it? People emit their emotional vibrations both good and bad.

Let's talk about sending good vibrations. Similar to the "forgive and forget" exercise, you can pray for people or send them positive thoughts and feelings. When we send out positive thoughts and feelings to others, they tend to return similar thoughts and feelings toward us. Send out sincere love and appreciation to others and they feel good about us. Send out disdain, anger, or resentment toward others, and they won't tend to warm up to us.

People can feel your positive energy and positive thoughts and they will return positive thoughts and energy to you, in kind. You can prove this to yourself!

Here's what you do. Every time you greet a person, look into their eyes and smile at them with real caring. In your mind (not out loud) say with feeling, "I love you, I'm really glad to see you today!" Remember you just say this in your mind!

Practice this little technique for the next couple of days and see what happens. You will be absolutely amazed at how your relationships with others improve.

That's all you have to do. Every time you greet someone just look them in the eyes, give a sincere smile, and in your mind (and from your heart) send them love! If you want to amplify this and keep it going beyond the greeting, try the following…

To maximize the good vibes you send out toward others and incline people to automatically like you, do the following…

1. Only talk about things that are of interest to the other person.
2. Occasionally give them a sincere compliment. Just try to notice things you like about them and tell them so.
3. Use the person's first name throughout your conversations with them.

4. Encourage them to talk about themselves and the things they like.

5. Make it your goal to focus on others and to treat each person you meet as if they are the most important person in the world.

If you follow these suggestions you'll send out very powerful positive energy towards others and they will love being around you! Try it you'll like it! Not only can these techniques boost your success in your job search, it will boost all your interactions with others in all areas of your life!

Proper Care and Feeding For A Job Winning Mindset

Successful people regularly feed their minds a diet of good positive messages, and they avoid pessimistic messages as much as possible. To increase your own success make sure you continually feed your mind with good positive messages about yourself, others, and about your future.

Do not listen to the news. Do not watch the news. Do not get involved in negative conversations. Do not get involved in subjects that cause negative emotions in you. Do not hang out with negative focused people (as much as possible). Stop finding fault with other people and with the situations in your life.

The easiest way to stop doing all the things listed in the last paragraph is to focus on feeding your mind with positive things. So...do listen to uplifting music, positive people, and positive attitude CDs, read positive books, and find things to do that you enjoy doing. Start focusing only on the good you can find in other people and in every situation around you.

Focusing on the positive takes a conscious effort. You must be aware of when you're thinking negatively and quickly decide to think positively instead, it is a choice. The easiest way to know where your mind is focused is by noticing how you feel.

When you feel bad your mind is likely focused on something negative. If you feel good or even great, your mind is likely focused on something good. It's your choice and the mindset you choose will make a big difference in how your job search (and your life) unfolds for you. It will also make a very big difference in how others feel about you.

Remember to avoid negative crud like the plague. Whatever you can find to feed your mind that is positive, do it, as often as possible.

Gain Altitude with Gratitude

A person can never feel good if they focus on what they don't have, or on what they don't like about their situation. However a person can always feel better when they focus on the things they are grateful for.

Gratitude as you can imagine goes right in line with feeding your mind positive things. Here is another very powerful way to keep your mind positive…

Make a list of everything you're grateful for, review the list every day and add to it every day. When you find a way to be grateful for what you already have you prepare yourself to receive more.

Usually a gratitude list starts out with the really big things like having a home to live in, having food, having clothes, having a friend, or family… and it works its way down to being grateful for toothpaste, socks, underwear and other essentials. Once you start your list you'll be surprised how many things you really are glad you have in your life, even simple things.

If you have a tough time thinking of things to be grateful for, you can try doing these things…

- Go visit the terminally ill ward at a children's hospital.
- Go visit elderly people in an old people's home.
- Go visit homeless people down on the streets or at your local homeless shelter.
- Do an exhaustive study on your favorite impoverished or war-torn nation, maybe Sudan or Haiti. Look for articles and pictures about starving children, ruthless dictators… you get the idea.

Then go write down everything you're grateful for in your life and add to the list every day, review this list every day. This is a great method for attitude adjustment and it helps you see things more clearly. It helps you be grateful for the many things you do have, and a grateful person is much more fun to be around than someone who is ungrateful and negative about life.

As you can imagine, hiring managers love to be around grateful uplifting people too.

Mental Emotional Image Projection (Daily)

Now here's a very powerful method for creating a job winning persona. Every morning before you get out of bed and each night before you go to sleep from now until you find your next job, do this...

As you lay on your bed both in the evening and in the morning, imagine yourself going through the winning job search process and landing a job. Imagine it as if it's really real.

See yourself having the best possible resume and cover letter that any manager has ever seen. Imagine yourself answering the phone and being invited to an interview at an awesome company. Imagine yourself as positive, upbeat, and confident in your interview.

See yourself as getting along fabulously with the hiring manager and everyone else at the company. Then see yourself accepting a new fantastic job with the new company! Feel excited about it, feel happy about it and enjoy all the wonderful feelings as if it is absolutely real. See and feel yourself getting your first nice paycheck from them!

Now remember to do this exercise before you go to sleep and before you get up every day. Promise yourself that you won't get out of bed until you do this exercise every morning. Promise? Ok!

This little exercise in itself will make a huge difference. Don't worry about the results of the previous day or the results of the next day, or the results of today.

Go ahead and do this wonderful exercise every night before you go to sleep and every morning before you get up. Very soon, it will become your reality!

Program Your Mind For Success

Now this one may seem a little weird but it does work. In fact it works pretty well for a lot of people.

There are 2 great ways to do this mind programming exercise and I personally use both. Go ahead and try both and see which one works better for you! Then just stick with the one that's easiest for you to do! Here's all you do…

<u>WARNING</u>: *Do not do the following exercises if you are prone to seizures unless you consult your doctor first and receive the ok to use them.*

Option 1: Stare at yourself in a mirror (look yourself straight in the eyes) for about 1 to 3 minutes each night before you go to sleep and repeat the 3 phrases listed on the next page over and over (preferably out loud) again for the full 1 to 3 minutes (say it in your mind if you have to). Say these phrases as a command to yourself with real power, conviction, and confidence!

Option 2: Stare at the image on the next page for about 1 to 3 minutes each night before you go to sleep, with a smile on your face, repeat the 3 phrases listed on the next page over and over (preferably out loud) again for the full 1 to 3 minutes (say it in your mind if you have to, but make sure you do this). Say these phrases as a command to yourself with real power, conviction, and confidence!

Try this exercise for the next 7 days and feel your confidence grow each day!

I AM JUST AS DESERVING AS EVERYONE ELSE!

I "CAN" HAVE MY IDEAL JOB!

I AM POSITIVE, CONFIDENT, CHARMING AND FUN!

Congratulations! If you've gone through every exercise outlined in this chapter you'll have built the foundation for a powerful job winning attitude.

Here are a few suggestions going forward. These are some quick hitters you can do every day to keep your mind sharp and positive as you finalize your job search and gain that new job.

Do the following, first thing every day till you find your new job…

1. Do a "what's bugging me now list" daily. (5 minutes)

2. Do the "forgive and forget exercise" daily. (5 minutes)

3. Do the "feed your mind a positive diet exercise" daily. (Throughout the day)

4. Review and add to your "gratitude list" daily. (5 minutes)

5. Do the send "positive vibes exercise" in all your interactions with others, daily. (Throughout the day)

6. "Visualize your job search success two times per day", morning and evening. (3 – 5 min each)

7. Program your mind to help you find that job! (3 minutes)

When you set the time aside each day to do these few exercises, not only will you find a job more quickly, your whole life will feel much better. Enjoy!

CHAPTER 2 - Identify Your Top Job Targets

Have you ever wondered what you could be doing to enjoy more personal fulfillment, success, and happiness in your career? When you begin to do what you are meant to do, all these things fall into place. I'm so glad I took the time to figure this out in my own life.

Now I'm enjoying greater success doing what I am designed to do. I've written books, began speaking to inspire others, improved my relationships with others, enjoyed greater career success, started my own corporation, and so much more. Most of all I've been pursuing my passion of helping more people to transform their lives and reach their dreams!

Life is so much more fun, so much more rewarding, so much more satisfying when you do what you are intended to do.

Did you know that you are actually designed to be very successful at something? In this section you will identify exactly what that something is by pinpointing your interests, your natural talents, your likes and dislikes, your skills, and so on.

First we will identify the ideal career for you, your ultimate dream job. Next we will identify other jobs you could be good at. Finally we will identify jobs you could do if you had to.

The reason this is important is that it gives you more options for jobs to go after for now as you move toward the ideal. If you just limit yourself to one job, depending on what that one job is, it could take you much longer than you want to find a job.

Simply go through all the exercises on the next few pages. When you've completed them you'll be able to identify a number of great jobs you can target to go after right away.

To get started ask yourself the following questions and write down your answers.

7 Powerful Self Exploration Questions

As you begin identifying the best career for you, it's important to examine who you really are and what you really desire. We will start this self examination process by tapping into your subconscious mind to help you gain clarity.

To do this you need to ask yourself the right questions. You'll begin this assessment by asking yourself 7 powerful self exploration questions that will help you discover the ideal work for you.

All you have to do right now is relax, clear you mind, then "read" each question on the next few pages and write down your initial answers on a separate piece of paper. Once you've answered these 7 questions you will move on to your "Career Assessment".

Continue to go through each assessment in this chapter until you have your top set of great jobs to go after! This exercise will give you more options for potential jobs, and it will help you gain insight into what you should ultimately be doing to be more successful.

7 Key Questions You Must Ask Yourself

1. As far back as you can remember (ages 1-5,ages 5-10, ages 10-15…) up to the present – what are you doing when you're having the most fun:

2. As far back as you can remember (ages 1-5, ages 5-10, ages 10-15…) up to the present – what are you doing when you're having the least fun (these are the types of things you want to avoid going forward):

3. As far back as you can remember what activities give you the most energy and get you excited?

4. What do you get most excited learning and talking about?

5. Going Back as far as you can remember (ages 1-5, ages 5-10, ages 10-15…) up to the present, and list all the things you do really well? List everything you are the best at doing:

6. Review everything you've written down above. Then, ask yourself "what could I be doing for a living that would fill me with excitement and passion, that would be very meaningful to me, that would provide value to others, and that someone would be willing to pay me to do?"

NOTE: Don't put a lot of pressure on yourself and don't worry if you don't seem to get a complete picture right away. Most will find profound answers very quickly, for others it may take a few days. Not a problem. If you don't get a lot of clarity right away try the following. Read your list of summarized answers (above) before you go to bed every night for the next 7 nights. Ask yourself the 6th question (above) and the 7th question (below) before you go to sleep. The answers will come. Don't be surprised when you wake up in the middle of the night with some exciting insights. Once you've received answers to these questions, you'll have found not only the ideal career for you, but a personal life mission you can really get passionate about.

7. Next ask yourself this question, "Considering my current obligations, responsibilities, and circumstances, what could I be doing right now in my current environment that would fill me with excitement and passion, that would be very meaningful to me, that would provide value to others, and that would move me toward my ultimate career goal?

Now Let's Gain Even More Clarity

By now there's a good chance you already have some ideas about what you could be doing for your ideal career, and ideas about other jobs you could do. However, be sure to go ahead and complete the additional assessments outlined in the remainder of this chapter.

By the time you're finished you'll be super clear about what jobs you want to go after to give you the greatest number of opportunities to land a great job fast.

Your Career Assessment

A good career assessment can give you awesome feedback about your greatest areas of career interest. I have provided links to several excellent free career assessments below for your convenience. I personally recommend both of these to my clients and employees. They both provide solid career feedback you can use.

NOTE: I have done all the research for you and found some of the best free career assessments available on the net, the links to them are provided further down on this page. However, there are a number of other good no-cost career assessments available on the Internet. You can find them by going to www.google.com and doing a search on the term "free career assessment".

To get started go to the link below, sign up, and take the free career test offered at this site. In about 20 minutes you will have a report that outlines your top career area interests along with other valuable information.

LINK: http://www.free-career-test.com/learnmore/main.asp

NOTE: Another very quick and easy FREE Career Assessment I can recommend is at http://similarminds.com/career.html . Feel free to give this one a try as well!

After you complete this career assessment and have summarized your results on the next page you can move on to the next assessment.

Summarize Your Career Assessment Results Below:

Your Temperament "Personality" Assessment

A good personality assessment will reveal to you what type of position you are best suited for in any given career field. Once you've identified your career areas of interest as you did in the previous section, you need to know how your personality fits in with your career interests. The Personality assessment you take in this section will do just that.

There are a number of good no-cost personality assessments available on the Internet. You can find them by going to www.google.com and doing a search on the term "free personality assessment" or "free personality test" to find one. Below I have provided a link to my favorite no-cost personality assessment, the "Keirsey Temperament Sorter".

When you are ready just go to the link below, sign up, and take this free Keirsey Temperament Sorter Assessment. In about 20 minutes you will have a report that outlines your personality type.

LINK: *http://www.keirsey.com/sorter/instruments2.aspx?partid=0*

After you complete this assessment and have summarized your results on the next page, go ahead and move on to the next step.

Summarize Your Keirsey Temperament Assessment Results Below:

What You Do Best!

In the space below write-down everything you're really good at doing. These are the types of things other people have complemented you on. Maybe someone has said, "hey you're really good at…", or "you really did a great job at…", and so on.

Maybe you're good at explaining things, writing, drawing, math, horseback riding, problem-solving, making friends, designing things, organizing things…It could also be something you received an award or recognition for. Just write down the types of things you are good at doing.

I Am Good At…(write down everything that comes to mind below):

Your Skills, Natural Talents, Training and Education, and Job Experience

Write down any Special Skills you may have here:

Write down any Natural Talents you may have here:

Write down any type of Training or Education you have here:

List any type of Job experience (that you like) you have here:

Now simply read through everything you've written down on the previous pages in this chapter. Review your answers to the first seven self exploration questions. Review your career assessment results and your personality assessment results. Review what you do best, your skills, natural talents, training and education, and job experience.

And Your Top Job Targets Are!

Now just answer the questions below…

What would be an Ideal Career For Me and what are the Top Jobs I should go after (my ultimate career)?

What other Good Jobs can I go after with a good chance of winning (other jobs I would be good at)?

What other Jobs could I do if I had to for a while?

Outstanding! You now have a solid list of jobs to target for your job search.

Now that you have your list of jobs to target in your job search, you're ready to begin preparing a job-getting resume. Armed with the wonderful insights you've gained in this chapter, you'll have some great information to use in building your resume! Congratulations!

CHAPTER 3 - Your Interview-Getting Cover Letter and Resume

Winning the Game of Resume Roulette

Your resume and cover letter exist for only one purpose, getting an interview!

It doesn't matter what you, your family, or your friends think about your resume. The only thing that does matter is that you have a resume that gets into the hiring managers hands and compels him or her to want to interview you as soon as possible. That's the goal.

Mountains of resumes and cover letters pour into companies each day. Most of them (often over 90%) never make it to the hiring manager. In this chapter you'll discover how to get your resume to the top of that resume mountain. You'll find out exactly how to write your resume to get it in front of more hiring managers and motivate them to want to interview you.

Getting Past The First Screening

It's kind of scary, but a lot of companies now use some type of automated program to review initial resumes. The goal of these programs is to screen out the vast majority of resumes that do not closely match the open position. You could be the perfect match for the job, but if your resume does not have enough of the right "key words" the program is looking for, you'll be screened out.

Your first challenge is to get past the first screening and have your resume selected for the hiring manager to review. Your second challenge is to have the hiring manager take one look at your resume and instantly put you at the top of his or her "must interview" list!

So here's where you start…

The Right Keywords and Buzzwords for Your Job and Industry

Keywords and key phrases are specific words and phrases that describe your skills and experience. They often include common buzzwords from your particular industry. For example a person looking for a management position may need to use words and phrases like "change management" or "organizational leadership". Someone in the writing field may use specific phrases or words such as "copywriter", "business writer" or "technical writer"…any words or phrases used in a job description for a particular job.

These keywords and phrases are very important. If you don't have enough of the right key phrases and key words in your resume, it will usually be thrown out without a chance.

So how do you find the best key words, phrases, and buzzwords for your career field to use in your resume? Here's all you do…

Go to any job search engine on the Internet, careerbuilder.com, monster.com, or one of my favorites, www.indeed.com , and search for jobs that match your skill set. For example…if you are a nurse search for nursing jobs, if you're a truck driver search for truck driver jobs, if you're an IT manager search for IT manager positions… and so on.

- Look over the jobs that are posted in your career field, especially for your type of position, and see what types of common phrases and words are used in these job postings. Make a list of the top key words, key phrases, and industry buzz words and include any that are applicable in your resume.
- Research industry trends, professional web sites, associations, magazines, and determine what keywords and buzzwords are commonly used. Apply any of these that make sense in your resume.
- Some additional phrases you may also see are things like strategic planning, productivity improvement, problem-solving, decision-making, team building…any phrases that appear to be commonly used in relation to job positions in your industry. Be sure to select only the ones that apply to jobs you are targeting and include these phrases in your resume.

Where to Place Keywords in Your Resume

You should always place keywords and phrases at the beginning of your resume. If you have a career summary section at the top of your resume this is a great place for them. The main idea is to put your top skills and experience, using keywords and phrases, where they will be noticed. This is usually at the beginning of your resume.

You'll also want to apply keywords and phrases in any areas of your resume that highlight your experience and abilities, such as your job descriptions and your job history.

Also any area of your resume that focuses on your greatest strengths, you'll want to use keywords and phrases there as well.

It's good to use between 10 and 20 keywords and phrases throughout your resume. This will give you a better chance of being selected by an automated screener, or by a human screener for that matter.

After your resume gets by the initial screening, it will be read by a hiring manager, so don't just cram a bunch of keywords and phrases into a resume to the point where it sounds unnatural.

You want your resume to be pleasing, factual, impressive, and professional, so use keywords only where it makes sense. Don't forget to add a few key phrases in your cover letter as well!

This is a lot easier than it sounds, trust me. Don't worry I'll walk you step-by-step through building your interview getting resume and cover letter in just a moment.

Spice It Up With Compelling Power Words

After you identify all the key words to use in your resume, you'll want to be sure to use power words to describe what you've done in your previous jobs. If used properly (and not overused) power words always make a great impression.

Here are some examples of great power words to use. Simply add some of these power words (where it makes sense) to your resume and cover letter, especially in your job history and skill descriptions (just sprinkle them throughout your cover letter and resume). You'll be amazed how nicely they spice things up for you!

Leadership

- Advanced
- Revitalized
- Directed
- Drove
- Achieved
- Headed
- Organized
- Inspired
- Motivated

Initiative

- Developed
- Set Up
- Created
- Planned
- Initiated
- Started
- Communicated
- Established
- Generated

- Introduced

- Restructured

- Launched

Achievement

- Achieved

- Acquired

- Provided

- Attained

- Finalized

- Negotiated

- Effected

- Improved

- Produced

- Expanded

- Performed

- Succeeded

- Directed

- Improved

- Verified

- Implemented

- Accomplished

- Exceeded

Problem Solving

- Analyzed

- Assessed

- Solved

- Explored

- Eliminated

- Revised

- Reduced

- Identified

- Undertook

- Updated

- Reviewed

- Resolved

- Reinforced

- Streamlined

- Simplified

- Inspected

Remember, use key words and phrases that pertain to the job or jobs you are targeting, and also use descriptive power words to describe yourself, your skills and your accomplishments.

Now you're ready. Let's go ahead and build your interview-getting resume and cover letter right now. Just follow the instructions in this chapter and you'll start getting a lot more interviews very quickly.

Create Your Interview-Getting Resume

In this section I will walk you through every step of building your new powerful resume. Here's how it flows…

1. Example #1. We'll cover how to find the right key words and phrases for the job you're after. I'll show you where to find job postings for positions you're looking for and walk you through how to identify the best key words to use in your resume.

2. Example #2. We'll cover the top two resume styles you'll want to use. I'll show you how to apply the keywords and key phrases to these resumes, so you'll know how to create your own keyword rich resume. We'll also cover how to use power words in these examples. You'll see exactly what the finished resume (using keywords, key phrases, and power words) should look like to have the best shot at winning an interview.

3. Example #3. We'll provide you outlines for the top 2 types of resumes we recommend. Simply copy the outlines to create your resume templates. Fill in the templates with your key words and power words to create your own interview-getting resume. In the end

you'll have a perfectly formatted resume filled with
great keywords and power words. It will be easy for
any hiring manager to read and (when done well) will
compel them to want to interview you!

How To Use The Right Key Words and Phrases In Your Resume

EXAMPLE JOB POSTING FOR FACILITIES MANAGER

Here's an example of how to find the right keywords and key phrases for your resume. Now of course I don't know what job you're after, but this process works the same for any job. Just follow this example all the way through using the same steps for the particular job you are after. Here we go…

For this example let's pretend I was an experienced facilities manager looking for a job with a new company. Here's what I'd do…

First I would find several job postings for Facilities Management positions. The Facilities Management job posting listed below was found by searching for job openings on the internet.

To find it I went to www.indeed.com and typed in "facilities manager". I then selected the job posting below to use as an example.

Next on the job posting I highlighted many of the keywords and phrases this employer will be screening for, related to this Facilities Manager job.

You see, if your resume matches closely to a particular job posting, using the same types of keywords, it has a much higher chance of being selected for an interview. This is because companies usually screen resumes based on the requirements in the job posting description. They look for resumes that are the closest match. Makes sense right?

Every job type you search for (accountant, cashier, truck driver, manager, engineer, clerk, bus boy…) will have its own set of key words and phrases, and every employer will have their own variations of job specific key words and phrases.

Here's how you find the right keywords and phrases for any job…

EXAMPLE JOB POSTING: Now read through the following job posting for a Facilities Manager position and notice all the highlighted key words and phrases we find…

FAC - Facilities / Physical Security

XXXXXXXX

None

None

Falls Country, MN

The Facilities Manager is responsible for managing and maintaining the facility requests including but not limited to, acting as the liaison for the customer; coordinating with vendors/service providers, and providing construction Project Management in owned and leased facilities. Provide oversight for building maintenance issues and requests, maintaining HVAC supplemental equipment, troubleshooting office equipment, and supporting multiple SAIC internal organizations to assure continuity and smooth operation of the facility. The position requires a self motivated individual who is flexible in their work schedule to support and manage multiple buildings locate in MN, DC and MD. Traveling between office locations will be required.

Duties and Responsibilities
1. Coordinates the maintenance of facilities, and equipment, as appropriate to ensure optimum functionality; identifies, assesses and resolves building maintenance and usage problems
2. Reviews all incoming work order requests for accuracy, investigates scope to coordinate and/or perform the work through completion.
3. Coordinates with Security on physical access for vendors and service providers during normal business hours and after hours support.
4. Plans, and maintains budgets working with the financial administrator
5. Performs various administrative duties such as maintaining occupancy records and provide information to financial administrator.
6. Serves as liaison between facility operations and Property Management; recommends correction of deficiencies; coordinates remodeling activities, as appropriate to the position.
7. Ability to design, plan and manage construction projects in owned and leased facilities.
8. Provides technical support and oversight in the management of estimates, bid sheets, layouts and construction contracts.
9. Coordinates office moves and performs minor office moves i.e. moving of boxes, furniture and fixtures
10. Performs miscellaneous job-related duties as assigned

Qualifications
• A minimum of 10 years work experience in facilities management
• Management in high rise class "A" buildings

• Need to be customer-service driven
• Ability to work and think independently
• Must be professional, punctual and reliable
• Must be well organized and have excellent verbal and written communication skills
• Must have good time management and project management accounting skills
• Ability to organize, prioritize, multitask and coordinate a range of tasks and responsibilities
• Must be able to demonstrate continuous effort to improve operations, decrease turnaround times, streamline work processes and work cooperatively and jointly to provide quality seamless customer service.

Education

A Bachelor's degree preferred, but comparable accomplishments in MEP and construction will be considered.

Key words and phrases are simply the words and phrases the employer uses to describe the skills they are looking for. Keep in mind you don't have to have every exact skill they are looking for. They may ask for 10 years hands on experience, and you may only have 8. That's ok. Just remember for any skills you do have, match their key words and key phrases as best you can.

Of course you'll want to add any other relevant information that pertains to your job or industry into your own resume. Just be sure to sprinkle your resume with key words and phrases that match any job postings you are applying for. This will greatly increase your chances of getting an interview! Oh, and don't forget to use a few power words too!

IMPORTANT: Other Things Employers Look For

Okay here's another important point. Yes employers are looking for the right keywords and phrases, and of course power words grab their attention. But what else do employers look for in your resume and cover letter? Grammar, punctuation, and spelling! That's right you can't get away from good grammar and good spelling.

Be sure your resume and cover letter are your best writing work. If you're not particularly good with grammar and spelling (like me!), make sure you find someone who can review your resume and cover letter before sending them out.

Also remember that your resume is a working document. First build a base or general resume that represents your experience, training, and skills. Then customize this base resume for specific jobs you find posted. In other words, for any job posting you apply for, you should customize your resume to match closely to each individual job posting when it makes sense to do so.

Of course you can send your base resume out to large numbers of employers as is. But whenever you find a specific job opening you want to go after, you'll do much better if you customize your resume to match that job posting as closely as possible.

The Top 2 Ways to Format Your Resume for Maximum Results:

I recently heard of a study that asked employers what type of resumes they preferred most. The top two formats by far are the chronological resume, and the skills based resume, and preferably a combination of both.

This makes complete sense of course because both of these resume types summarize your skills and your experience in a simple easy-to-read format, and that's what employers want.

Ease, speed, and pertinent information, keep these three things in mind as you create your resume. Here's what I mean...

As a hiring manager I absolutely dislike having to go through long winded resumes that are hard to follow. As a general rule, hiring managers don't have a lot of extra time so they really love to see a well written resume.

A resume that's quick and easy to read, and tells them exactly what they want to know. What do hiring managers really want to know? Basically they want to know the following things from your Resume...

- Can you do the job (are you qualified) or can you learn it?
- Will you do a good job?
- Can you hit the ground running or will you need a lot of training?
- What unique value can you bring to the organization?
- Are you a self-starting go getter?
- Are you credible, trustworthy, dependable, and hard working?
- Are you the type who goes the extra mile?
- Do you get along well with others?

I always tell my current employees that the only job security they have is between their ears. If they have good character, if they are excellent at what they do, if they have a great attitude, if they get along with others, if they're dependable, trustworthy, and hard-working, who would ever want to let them go?

The same goes for hiring. If a person is capable of these types of qualities, they'll have a much better chance of landing a job quickly.

If indeed you are capable of these qualities, and I think we all really are, make sure you convey them in some way shape or form in your resume and during your interview. Hiring managers just want someone to do a great job, who will get along well with others, and who won't be a pain in the #@!! to manage!

Resume Examples Using These Techniques

On the following pages are two sample resumes that use the right keywords for the job they are after. Both are sprinkled with power words to make them more dynamic. In the examples below, the job or industry keywords are highlighted in light grey and the power words highlighted with a darker highlight.

The first resume is for an experienced worker, and the second resume is more for an entry-level or just out of school worker. Go ahead and view the sample resumes below to see how you can put yours all together.

<u>Andrew A. Dude</u>
1234 South 234th Ave, Omaha, NE 68144
Home: (808) 555-1111 – Cell: (808) 666-2222 – Email:
adude@mail.com

Objective: Position as a Facilities Manager

HIGHLIGHTS OF QUALIFICATIONS

- 8 years of hands-on facilities management experience

- Very strong coordination and communication skills (both verbal and written)

- Experienced at handling maintenance requests for high rise class "A" buildings

- Experienced at troubleshooting HVAC and other office equipment issues

- Professional independent worker with outstanding customer service skills

- Organized and able to multitask by using good time management skills

- Enjoy my work immensely and always strive to contribute wherever I can

RELEVANT EMPLOYMENT & EXPERIENCE

1996 - Present: Facilities Manager – Big Buildings Inc., **Long Island, NY**

Facilities Management Skills and Experience

- Streamlined maintenance request and issue reporting process, improving response times by an average of 4 hours per request.
- Improved operations by optimizing maintenance schedules to reduce production downtime and increase equipment uptime, efficiency, and reliability.
- Decreased turnaround times for troubleshooting HVAC and other office equipment issues by implementing efficient best practice troubleshooting procedures.
- Reduced outside maintenance costs by 35% by negotiating new contracts with our existing venders and service providers.
- Developed improved methods for providing quality customer service, increasing customer satisfaction ratings by 22%.
- Successfully kept our facilities running smoothly and met all necessary regulations by operating an efficient and organized maintenance strategy.

Coordination and Project Management Skills and Experience

- Reviewed work order requests, investigated and validated the scope of work, and coordinated the completion of work for each request.
- Coordinated orders and deliveries of all vendor and service provider equipment and services.
- Performed project management oversight for all facilities projects including full building expansion projects and all building remodels.
- Coordinated with Security to provide physical building access to vendors and 3rd party providers.

Planning and Organizing Skills and Experience

- Worked closely with the financial administrator to plan and maintain effective budgets.
- Designed, developed, and managed project plans for all construction projects including building expansion and remodels.
- Developed and implemented plans for improving customer service ratings, improving maintenance operations, and decreasing turnaround times for repairs.

1994-96 Facilities Assistant - Hunt Foundation, **Huntsville, TX**

Customer Service Skills
- As liaison for our customers, I managed and maintained all facilities requests efficiently.
- Reviewed incoming work requests and coordinated the completion of all work requests.
- Coordinated the maintenance of facilities and equipment for campus facilities.

Reading & Writing Skills
- Applied rapid reading techniques to stay on top of industry trends listed in trade magazines and articles.
- Studied facilities management best practice guides to glean new improvement ideas for our facilities.
- Developed and wrote improved troubleshooting procedures, and improved customer satisfaction surveys, gaining valuable feedback from customers in order to improve our service delivery.

EDUCATION

B.A. Facilities Management, Honors, Brigham Young University, 1994

M.A. Business Management, Long Island University, 1996

Andrew A. Dude

1234 South 234th Ave, Omaha, NE 68144 - Home (808) 555-1111 -
Cell (808) 666-2222

adude@mail.com

Objective: Position as a Facilities Management Assistant

HIGHLIGHTS OF QUALIFICATIONS

- 2 years of hands-on facilities management experience as an Intern

- Very strong coordination and communication skills (both verbal and written)

- Knowledgeable in handling maintenance requests

- Professional independent worker with outstanding customer service skills

- Organized and able to multitask by using good time management skills

RELEVANT SKILLS & EXPERIENCE

Facilities Management Skills and Experience
- Successfully researched and developed improved facilities operations methods in class room assignments using the most up to date facilities management best practice methods.
- Quality Customer service experience as an intern at xyz company.
- Experienced at coordinating vendor and service provider deliveries.
- Reviewed work order requests, investigated and validated the scope of work.

Organizational Skills

- Utilized Microsoft Project in class to develop construction project management project plans. Designed, planned, and managed large scale mock projects in class, tracking task management, issue logs, mile stone completion, and project budgets.

Reading & Writing Skills

- Utilized accelerated reading skills to study numerous facilities management best practice guides to glean new improvement ideas for our facilities.

- Wrote numerous procedure improvement plans during course work including, customer service improvement procedures, troubleshooting best practice procedures, and building maintenance best practice procedures.

EMPLOYMENT & INTERNSHIP HISTORY

2006-Present Facilities Assistant – Small Shops, Kansas City, KS

EDUCATION

A.A. Facilities Management, Kansas State College, 2006

So what's the square box with the initials at the top left for?

Hey, glad you noticed! That's one of the little tricks to getting your resume to stand out from all the other thousands of resumes that flood a hiring company. The square box with your first and last initials, make your resume different than all those others that flood the company. Once you're past any electronic screeners, a human screener will notice the initials, take a closer look, and often select your resume out of the crowd just because it's so clean, concise, and it stands out as different!

IMPORTANT: Use Concise Figures and Numbers for Greatest Impression

Notice also that in these resume examples, we use %. Like, increased productivity 25%. Or reduced delay by 15%...and so on. For some situations you may want to list dollars like, Increased Revenue by $200,000.00, or, saved the company $150,000.00 by...

Wherever you can, use numbers and percents to emphasize any results you have accomplished. When you do, it instantly boosts your credibility with potential employers. I don't think I need to say this, but please only state things that are 100% true. Just be sure to present them in the best light!

The Finished Product

On the following pages are the two example resumes without any highlights. They use all the right keywords and key phrases for the job they're going after, and they use great power words.

A few other things to notice about these resumes is that they are professional looking, short and to the point, and they cater to all the things a hiring manager wants to know. They also stand out from the rest of the resume crowd by having the initials in a box at the top right corner. Very few people are aware of, or use, this technique.

Excellent Resume Examples

Now go ahead and look at the two cleaned up resumes on the next few pages. After you review them I'll provide you a few final notes and give you the resume template/outlines you can use to create your outstanding resume. Simply model these templates and fill in the blanks. Of course you want to be original using the right power words for you and the right key words and phrases for your particular job target.

<u>Andrew A. Dude</u>
1234 South 234th Ave, Omaha, NE 68144
Home: (808) 555-1111 – Cell: (808) 666-2222 – Email:
adude@mail.com

Objective: Position as a Facilities Manager

HIGHLIGHTS OF QUALIFICATIONS

- 8 years of hands-on facilities management experience

- Very strong coordination and communication skills (both verbal and written)

- Experienced at handling maintenance requests for high rise class "A" buildings

- Experienced at troubleshooting HVAC and other office equipment issues

- Professional independent worker with outstanding customer service skills

- Organized and able to multitask by using good time management skills

- Enjoy my work and strive to contribute in whatever ways I can

RELEVANT EMPLOYMENT & EXPERIENCE

2006 - Present: Facilities Manager – Big Buildings Inc., **Long Island, NY**

Facilities Management Skills and Experience

- Streamlined maintenance request and issue reporting process, improving response times by an average of 4 hours per request.
- Improved operations by optimizing maintenance schedules to reduce production downtime and increase equipment uptime, efficiency, and reliability.
- Decreased turnaround times for troubleshooting HVAC and other office equipment issues by implementing efficient best practice troubleshooting procedures.
- Reduced outside maintenance costs by 35% by negotiating new contracts with our existing venders and service providers.
- Developed improved methods for providing quality customer service, increasing customer satisfaction ratings by 22%.
- Successfully kept our facilities running smoothly and met all necessary regulations by operating an efficient and organized maintenance strategy.

Coordination and Project Management Skills and Experience

- Reviewed work order requests, investigated and validated the scope of work, and coordinated the completion of work for each request.
- Coordinated orders and deliveries of all vendor and service provider equipment and services.
- Provided project management oversight for all facilities projects including full building expansion projects and all building remodels.
- Coordinated with Security to provide physical building access to vendors and 3rd party providers.

Planning and Organizing Skills and Experience

- Worked closely with the financial administrator to plan and maintain effective budgets.

- Designed, developed, and managed project plans for all construction projects including building expansion and remodels.
- Developed and implemented plans for improving customer service ratings, improving maintenance operations, and decreasing turnaround times for repairs.

2003-2006 Facilities Assistant - Hunt Foundation, **Huntsville, TX**

Customer Service Skills

- As liaison for our customers, I managed and maintained all facilities requests efficiently.
- Reviewed incoming work requests and coordinated the completion of all work requests.
- Coordinated the maintenance of facilities and equipment for campus facilities.

Reading & Writing Skills

- Applied rapid reading techniques to stay on top of industry trends listed in trade magazines and articles.
- Studied facilities management best practice guides to glean new improvement ideas for our facilities.
- Developed and wrote improved troubleshooting procedures, and improved customer satisfaction surveys, gaining valuable feedback from customers in order to improve our service delivery.

EDUCATION

Facilities Management Program, Huntsville Community College, 2002-2004

<u>Andrew A. Dude</u>

1234 South 234th Ave, Omaha, NE 68144 - Home (808) 555-1111 - Cell (808) 666-2222

adude@mail.com

Objective: Position as a Facilities Management Assistant

HIGHLIGHTS OF QUALIFICATIONS

- 2 years of hands-on facilities management experience as an Intern

- Very strong coordination and communication skills (both verbal and written)

- Knowledgeable in handling maintenance requests

- Professional independent worker with outstanding customer service skills

- Organized and able to multitask by using good time management skills

RELEVANT SKILLS & EXPERIENCE

Facilities Management Skills and Experience
- Successfully researched and developed improved facilities operations methods in class room assignments using the most up to date facilities management best practice methods.
- Customer service experience as an intern.
- Experience coordinating vendor and service provider deliveries.
- Reviewed work order requests and validated the scope of work.

Organizational Skills

- Utilized Microsoft Project in class to develop construction project plans. Designed planned and managed large scale mock projects in class, tracking tasks, issue logs, mile stone completion, and project budgets.

Reading & Writing Skills

- Utilized accelerated reading skills to study numerous facilities management best practice guides to glean new improvement ideas for our facilities.

- Wrote numerous procedure improvement plans during course work including customer service improvement procedures, troubleshooting best practice procedures, and building maintenance best practice procedures.

EMPLOYMENT & INTERNSHIP HISTORY

2006-Present Facilities Assistant – Small Shops, Kansas City, KS

EDUCATION

A.A. Facilities Management, Kansas State College, 2006

Putting Your Job Getting Resume Together

On the previous pages you've been given every bit of information you need to create an interview getting resume. Let's summarize here what you need to do.

#1. Go to www.indeed.com and look for job postings for the particular type of job you're going after.

#2. Print out several job postings for your type of job and highlight all the keywords and key phrases that these employers use. Use any common words and phrases in your general resume, and then tailor your resume for specific job openings by using the company specific keywords and phrases (the words they use in their job posting).

#3. Grab the list of power words shown earlier in this chapter (or think of your own power words) and highlight the type of power words you can use in your resume to describe your skills and experience.

#4. Choose the resume template example (format) that best suits your experience level and background.

#5. Create your resume based on the template or format you choose with all the right keywords and key phrases for the job you are after. Sprinkle power words throughout your resume to describe your skills, experience, and accomplishments.

#6. Check your resume for spelling and grammatical errors (and have someone else check it too). Then have at least three (honest) people review your resume and give you honest feedback. Look for any common things all three of them say about your resume. If all three didn't like something you may consider changing that something.

#7. Once you feel your resume is as good as you can get it, start sending it out to every job opening you can find (you'll be learning all about job search methods and techniques in the next chapter of this book). Be sure to have a base resume that covers everything pretty well for your type of job. Make customized resumes for any specific job postings you are applying for.

Excellent Resume Templates

Whenever you're ready to start on your resume, you can go to…
http://www.careersuccesstraining.com/docs/MDRusumeTemplates.docx

…and download these two resume templates. Or you can simply recreate the appropriate resume template/outline found on the next couple of pages and follow the directions outlined in this section. Before you know it you'll have one fantastic interview-getting-resume!

<u>Your Name – Resume Template 1</u>
Your Street Address, City, State, Zip Code
Home: (xxx) xxx-xxxx – Cell: (xxx) xxx-xxxx – Email:
xxxxx@xxxxx.com

Objective: Position as a ______________________

HIGHLIGHTS OF QUALIFICATIONS

- __ Years of hands-on ____ key words _________experience

- Very strong ___________ key words _____________ skills

- Experienced at _________ key words __________________

- Experienced at _________ key words __________________

- Professional independent worker with outstanding customer service skills

- Enjoy my work and strive to contribute in whatever ways I can

RELEVANT EMPLOYMENT & EXPERIENCE

Start Year – End Date or Present: Position Held – Company Name., **City, State**

______key words__________ Skills and Experience

- Streamlined _____key words _____________________________.
- Improved _______key words _____efficiency, and reliability.
- Reduced________ key words ____________________________.
- Developed ______ key words ___________________________.
- Successfully _____key words ___________________________.

_______key words__________ Skills and Experience

- Reviewed _______ key words ____________________________.
- Coordinated ______key words ___________________________.
- Provided _________key words ___________________________.
- Coordinate _______ key words __________________________.

Start Year – End Date or Present: Position Held – Company Name, **City, State**

________key words__________ Skills and Experience

- Worked closely with ______________key words_________.
- Designed, planned, and managed ______key words________.
- Developed and implemented _________key words ________.

EDUCATION (or Specialized Training)

B.A. ___Major___, __ University____, Year Graduated xxxx
M.A. . ___Major___, __ University____, Year Graduated xxxx

<u>Your Name – Resume Template 2</u>

Your Street Address, City, State, Zip Code

Home: (xxx) xxx-xxxx – Cell: (xxx) xxx-xxxx – Email: xx@xxxx.com

---

Objective: Position as a ________________

HIGHLIGHTS OF QUALIFICATIONS

- __ years of hands-on ____key words_________ experience

- Very strong ___________ key words _____________ skills

- Experienced at _________ key words ________________

- Knowledgeable in all aspects of _____ key words _________

- Professional independent worker with outstanding customer service skills

- Enjoy my work and strive to contribute in whatever ways I can

RELEVANT SKILLS & EXPERIENCE

___________key word_________ Skills and Experience

- Successfully researched and ____________________________.
- Customer service experience_______________________________.
- Experience____.
- Reviewed____.
- Created____.
- Organized____.

___________key word__________ **Skills and Experience**

- __________describe keyword skills here________________.
- __________describe keyword skills here________________.

___________key word__________ **Skills and Experience**

- __________describe keyword skills here________________.
- __________describe keyword skills here________________.

EMPLOYMENT & INTERNSHIP HISTORY

Start Year – End Date or Present: Position Held – Company Name, City, State

EDUCATION (or Specialized Training)

B.A. ___Major___, __ University____, Year Graduated xxxx
Certification ___Skill___, __ Training School____, Year Graduated

Building Your Job Winning Cover Letter

I remember the first time I received a really good cover letter from a job applicant. It grabbed my attention, peaked my interest, and automatically made me like the person who'd sent it!

A cover letter is another important part of your quest to gain an interview. What is a cover letter? Well it's simply a personalized introduction to your resume. Your resume shows your skills and experience relevant to the job. Your cover letter simply shows a little more of your personal side.

A great cover letter shares a little bit about your experience, a little bit more about your interest in the position in the company, and a lot more about your passion for what you do. Believe me hiring managers love workers who are passionate about their work.

First let's start out with a couple of standard cover letter formats. You can go to the following website link listed below to look at different samples of cover letters. Do not model these for your cover letter, because I will show you how to create a cover letter that really stands out. A cover letter that grabs the attention of both initial screeners and of hiring managers.

At the link below are a number of standard cover letters (there are some decent cover letters at this website link, but I'll show you how to make your cover letter even better).

http://www.quintcareers.com/cover_letter_samples.html

Feel free to use any of the cover letters you find at the above link as a starting point for your cover letter. You may want to print out several of them and highlight the things you like about each one. Grab ideas from those to use in your own cover letter.

When you've got a first draft of your cover letter completed, take a look at the following examples on the next few pages. You'll see they contain something most cover letters and resumes miss altogether, "Passion"!

That's right, passion. If you can demonstrate that you love what you do, this will set you apart from 95% of all other applicants. When you demonstrate that you are passionate about your work, hiring managers will definitely want to talk to you. People who are passionate about their work make the best employees in any environment. People who hate their job typically make the worst employees.

I'm not kidding about this. If everything else is equal on a cover letter or resume, the person who shows passion for what they do will have the clear advantage.

Here are some examples of how to add passion to your cover letter.

<u>Andrew A. Dude</u>
1234 South 234th Ave, Omaha, NE 68144
Home (808) 555-1111 - Cell (808) 666-2222 - adude@mail.com

January 3, 2012

Ms. Job Screener
Human Resource Director
Big Property Management Inc.
3333 FNB Drive, Suite 101
Sometown, USA 60131

Ms. Screener:

Available: Dynamic Facilities Manager with Strong Communication Skills and a Passion For Excellent Customer Service!

Over the years I have had the opportunity to hold several incredible managerial positions. I now look forward to applying my experience, knowledge, and skills where I can continue to grow and provide value in this field!

I hope you'll find that my qualifications for this management position are an ideal fit.

You'll find included in my resume, a wide-variety of skills and practical hands-on experience that will enable me to very effectively administer your company's operations and procedures. I possess exceptional communication skills which I believe are extremely important for any managerial position.

Not only do I possess the qualifications you want and expect in a successful manager, I also possess a <u>dedication to excellence!</u>

I am excited about the possibility of a personal interview at your earliest convenience to further discuss my credentials with you.

Best regards,

Andrew A. Dude

(Signature)

HM: 808-555-1111
CELL: 808-666-2222

P.S. Thank you in advance for your consideration for this position. I sincerely look forward to meeting with you soon!

Enclosure: Resume

Ursula C. Wonderbabe

333 South 34th Street, Big Town, NJ 68554
Home (505) 222-1111 - Cell (505) 333-2222 -
ucwonderbabe@mail.com

April 12th, 2012

Rob Hiremenow
Sr. Recruiter
Mega Computer Inc.
31440 Western Highway
Favorite Hills, USA 12345-1212

Dear Mr. Hiremenow,

I am immediately available and very interested in the Data Network Technical Consultant Position you have open.

For the past 4 years, I have gained highly valued expertise in the field of Network Technical Consulting, which I absolutely love. I am now looking forward to applying my experience, knowledge and skills in a new setting, where I can continue to grow in this field. In addition to my Data Network skills, my 7 years of experience with all aspects of project management will make me a valuable asset to both your company and your customers.

After recently researching **The Mega Computer Inc.** vision statement, I believe I can make an immediate and positive contribution to your bottom line. I can hit the ground running by delivering effective best practice solutions to your existing customers and help drive additional business for your company.

Data Network Consulting is a true passion for me; Understanding customer problems, providing recommendations for improvements, and providing data network technology solutions that support business objectives are what I do best!

I will follow-up with a phone call next week to make sure you have received my application and resume.

Sincerely,

Ursula Wonderbabe

P.S. *I would love the opportunity to discuss this position with you in detail. I can be contacted at (505) 333-2222 to schedule a time to meet with you. Thank you in advance!*

Enclosure: Resume

Just use the above examples and you'll have everything you need to create a powerful cover letter to compliment your great resume!

What About Using a CV Instead of A Resume?

Some people use a CV instead of a resume. A curriculum venue or CV is more often used by people in academic fields. You can follow all the same principles outlined in this chapter, using keywords, using power words and so on…

I don't claim to be an expert on CVs as I am not in the academic field. Keep in mind I was a ninth-grade dropout till the age of 27 and still don't have a college degree.

If your situation calls for the use of a CV, I suggest visiting the link below where there are a number of samples of excellent CVs.

You can take a look at those CV samples and then apply all the principals you've learned throughout this chapter. No doubt with the insider information you now have you'll stand a much better chance of landing an interview quickly.

CV Examples:

http://jobsearch.about.com/od/cvsamples/a/blsamplecv.htm

How To Get Your Cover Letter and Resume Critiqued By an Expert for Free!

This is a really cool technique I've used and found it to be super helpful! You know how you usually have a friend or family member review your resume and give you feedback? Now this can be helpful especially where grammar and spelling are concerned.

However it may not always be as helpful as it could be unless they review resumes for a profession, or they are a hiring manager or a recruiter. First off, they may be afraid to tell you what they really think. Or they may be too critical and focus on something that doesn't really matter to a hiring manager, or…

The point is, there is a better way to have a professional review your resume "for free" and give you feedback. Here are several ways you can do it…

- Free online resume review services (do a Google search for "free online resume review services").
- Call the contacts at companies you apply for and ask them if they would review it for you and give you feedback.
- Call local hiring managers and ask them for their honest feedback on your resume.
- Call local teachers at local colleges and ask them if they would review it and give you feedback!

What About References?

Employers spend a lot of time and money to hire and train new employees. I've seen estimates that it costs employers anywhere from 38% to 150% of an individual's annual salary just to hire, train, and get them productive.

There are advertising costs, time spent selecting, lost income from not being able to get the work done till someone is hired and trained, training time and cost…and so on. That would be a minimum of $11,400 or a maximum of $45,000 to hire and train a person who makes $30,000 per year. If that person doesn't work out, that's a $11,400 to $45,000 loss.

Employers take a risk and make an investment whenever they hire someone. So when you have great references, it helps put the hiring company at ease and makes it easier for them to want to hire you. Bad references on the other hand will usually kill your chances of getting in the door.

If you're like most people you probably have a few people who are glad to give you a good reference. Even if you're new to the world of work, you probably have teachers, neighbors, pastors, or someone who can give you a character reference.

Be sure to have references ready and send them along with your resume and cover letter when you apply for jobs. Also have them ready when you interview. This will definitely impress any potential employer because you have them and you're not afraid to give them!

All you have to do is go to the top people you know who are willing to write you a very positive reference and ask them to do so.

Some of the best people to ask for a reference are:

- Anyone with a big fancy title
- Anyone well known (with a good reputation)
- Former bosses and co-workers
- Former clients or customers
- People you've helped in the past
- Past teachers or educators
- Ministers
- Friends

If anyone you ask for a reference is not sure how to write a reference, you can point them to the following link. This is a great resource where they can find reference letter templates and other great ideas on how to write a great reference letter for you.

http://jobsearch.about.com/od/referenceletters/Sample_Reference_Letters.htm

Ok, that does it for this chapter!

You now have a great interview-getting resume, cover letter, and some great references.

In the next chapter, you'll discover the best ways to find a whole bunch of open jobs you can go after.

CHAPTER 4 - Amazingly Effective Job Search Secrets

Introduction to Effective Job Searching

Congratulations, to this point you've built a strong foundation for landing a job. You've been working every day on getting and maintaining a positive attitude. You've identified the best types of jobs you should go after and you've built a great key-word-rich resume that will land you more interviews. Now you just need to find where all the open jobs are, and that's just what we'll cover in this chapter.

As you get into your job search, you'll quickly find it's very easy to get lost in the process. You can find yourself spending too much time on job search methods that don't really work, and not enough time on the ones that will bring you the best results.

You've probably heard about all the ways to find a job using twitter, video resumes, Linked-In, job search engines, job boards, having your own blog…and on and on. Sure some of these will help, but some of these new methods can actually hurt your chances of getting a job if not used properly. What you really need are the most effective ways to find a job quickly, not things that consume your time and get you sidetracked.

In this section we cover the facts. You want a job fast right? Here I'll give you an effective job search strategy, a schedule to follow, and a method for job searching and following up that will help you land a job quicker than most other job hunters out there.

Before we dive into the job search you should have the following things already.

- You should know exactly what three to five jobs you are targeting for your job search (including your dream job, other jobs you can be good at, and jobs you can do if you have to).

- You should have your base resume and cover letter ready.

- You should have your head in the game and be totally focused on finding a job now.

Here are a few "Job Search Success Principles" that will help you get the best results during your job search…

Job Search Success Principles

1. **Take a personal inventory of yourself**. Create a list of all the things you can do that people will be willing to pay you for. Include all the things you've done especially well in your previous jobs. Know your value, know what you do best and be fully prepared to communicate your value with ease.

2. **Understand hiring company's needs in the current marketplace**. All jobs are subject to the economic law of supply and demand. Employers must want and need what you have to offer before they will consider hiring you. It's up to you to keep your knowledge and job skills up-to-date and in tune with what employers currently need.

3. **Go where the others don't and spread the word everywhere**. About 70% of available jobs aren't being advertised online or offline. Be willing to contact companies

directly and ask to speak to the hiring manager of the department you would work for. When you get the hiring manager, quickly (30 seconds or less) tell them about your skills and what your value to them is. Ask them how you may be able to help them and their company. Tell friends, family, and anyone who can potentially help you that you have great skills and you're looking for job. Spread the word everywhere!

4. **Make finding your next job more than a full-time job**. Many super successful people work more than 50 hours per week. Treat your job search like successful people treat their jobs, put extra effort, time, and focus into your job search.

5. **Follow up faster and better than anyone else**. Whenever you talk live with a recruiter, a human resource person or hiring manager in a company where you are trying to get a job, follow up immediately with a hand written "Thank You" note letting them know how much you enjoyed meeting them and that you truly appreciate their time. If you have applied for a position or sent a resume to a company (and have not heard back), follow up with them one to two weeks later with a note affirming your interest in working for them.

6. **Go to work for them before you start**. When you get a first interview with any company, at the end of your first interview ask them what some of the greatest challenges are for the position and department you are applying for. Then tailor your responses in your remaining interviews toward helping them solve their challenges. Solution finders are valuable.

How Long Will It Take To Get A Job?

If You Want To Land A Job Fast - Here's What Your Calendar Should Look Like (as close to this as possible):

Finding and landing a job is partially a numbers game. The more time and effort you put into finding job openings, sending out resumes, calling companies, and following up, the sooner you will win that new job!

Just spend as many hours per day as you can (up to 8 hours per day) searching for jobs, sending out resumes and following up! Doing this will keep you busy so you worry less about finding a job and it will move you closer and closer to your new job!

Keep doing your daily practice of building and maintaining your job-winning mindset (what you learned in chapter one). You'll need it so you don't fall into discouraging crud thinking that won't serve you. Keep your mindset good and you will realize that it's only a matter of time before you have your new job. The more time and effort you apply each day, every day, the quicker your job will appear!

Here's what you should strive to model your calendar after, (as close to this as possible) to get a job faster…

30 Full Days of Job Searching: 8 hrs. per day x 30 days = 240 hours

Monday	Tuesday	Wednesday	Thursday	Friday
Job Search 8 hours	Job Search 8 hours	Job Search 8 hours	Job Search 8 hours	Job Search 8 hours

The point is to actually treat your job search more seriously than most people treat their job! When you focus 8 hours per day, 5 days per week on getting a job, using the cool insider tips you've gained and are gaining from this book, you "Will" get a job fast!

Your Daily Job Search Schedule

Rubber meets the road here! Only action will get you a job, and only the right action will get you one faster! Here are a couple of example daily schedules to help you understand how you want to focus your time....

IMPORTANT NOTE: Be sure to set daily goals. For example some good targets would be to make contacts with at least 10 new companies per day, or to send out at least 10 resumes per day. Obviously the more you can do each of these every day, the better! It is a numbers game!

Daily Schedule First Week

Time	Tasks	Notes:
08:00	Mental Fitness Preparation	1. Visualize accepting a great job offer. 2. Clear out mental clutter. 3. Fill up with positive influences 4. Surrender the situation and get to work. 5. Review your resume and think about all you have to offer your new employer.
08:30	Call Companies Direct	
09:00	Call Companies Direct	
09:30	Call Companies Direct	
10:00	Break – Refresh Mind and Body	
10:30	Search Job Openings	
11:00	Search Job Openings	
11:30	Search Job Openings	
Lunch		
1:00	Send Resumes	
2:00	Send Resumes	
2:30	Send Resumes	
3:00	Break – Refresh Mind and Body	
3:30	Search Job Openings	
4:00	Call Companies Direct	
4:30	Contact Friends, Family, Job Support Groups…	
5:00	Go Do Something Fun!	

Daily Schedule After First Week (with follow up)

Time	Tasks	Notes:
08:00	Mental Fitness Preparation	1. Visualize accepting a great job offer. 2. Clear out mental clutter. 3. Fill up with positive influences 4. Surrender the situation and get to work. 5. Think about all you have to offer your new employer.
08:30	Call Companies Direct	
09:00	Call Companies Direct	
09:30	Follow Up Calls	
10:00	Break – Refresh Mind and Body	
10:30	Search Job Openings	
11:00	Search Job Openings	
11:30	Follow Up Calls	
Lunch		
1:00	Send Resumes	
2:00	Send Resumes	
2:30	Send Resumes	
3:00	Break – Refresh Mind and Body	
3:30	Search Job Openings	
4:00	Call Companies Direct	
4:30	Follow Up Calls	
5:00	Go Do Something Fun!	

Mental Preparation – Daily Job-Getting Success Ritual

When you look at the example daily job schedules above, you'll notice the first thing to focus on each day is mindset. The single most important thing you can do as you job search is to stay mentally fit. We addressed this in the first chapter, but I think it's important to reemphasize this again as you start your job search.

Almost all super successful people practice a daily ritual. Successful entrepreneurs, successful business people, successful athletes, you name it. Successful people rehearse their success in advance, in their minds. For whatever reason it really works!

Success rituals have been responsible for much of my own personal and financial success. But don't just believe me because I'm saying this, prove it to yourself! Every day from now until you land your next job, practice the following ritual…

You should practice the following success ritual every evening before you go to bed and every morning first thing after you wake up.

1. **Visualize yourself accepting a great job offer from a great company**. Just get in a very relaxed state before you doze off to sleep at night and imagine yourself at the perfect company, sitting in an office. Across from you is your new boss handing you a fantastic new job offer and welcoming you to the company! See your new boss as very excited to hire you and feel yourself feeling the excitement and the happiness of getting a fantastic job offer! Imagine the scene as vividly as you can, using all five senses. See the sights of the situation, smell the smells of the room, feel the feelings of the situation, hear

the sounds of the room, and even taste the tastes of being in this situation. The point is to make it as a real as you possibly can in your imagination. This visualization when you first wake up and before you get out of bed each morning. Visualization is a powerful tool used by the world's most successful people. You'll see exactly why as you do this daily, until you get your next job.

2. **Write a "what's bugging me now list".** Every morning after you get out of bed write out a "what's bugging me now" list. Take out some blank pieces of paper and draw two lines to divide the paper into 3 columns. Write down at the top of the piece of paper, "what's bugging me now?" Then in the far left column write down everything that's worrying you, everything that's bothering you, everything that makes you angry, everything that makes you sad…just write down everything that comes to mind that's bugging you. It can be fear of job hunting, it can be doubts, it can be your spouse or your children bugging you, it can be people you talk to on the phone that are rude, it can be worries about finances… It should be everything that's bothering you at that moment. Then in the second column, next to each thing that bothers you write down why it bothers you. Maybe it hurt your feelings, maybe you're afraid, maybe you're angry….then in the third column, write-down anything positive you can do about it. Maybe you can forgive someone, maybe you can learn to accept the situation and focus on doing your best anyway, maybe you can make amends to someone if you did something wrong. Just write down any positive thing you can do about each situation. That's it. Once you write-down your what's bugging me now list, you'll find you feel an incredible sense of freedom. You'll feel great! Try It!

3. **Create a "gratitude list" and add to it every day**. Take
    out a blank sheet of paper and write-down at the top of it,
    "I am grateful for…" Then write down everything you can
    think of that you are grateful for. Food, a place to sleep,
    friends, family, talents, skills, education, socks, shoes,
    underwear, toilet paper, a place to take a shower, soap,
    toothpaste, toothbrush…write down everything you can
    think of that makes your life better. Every day review this
    gratitude list after you do your "what's bugging me now
    list". Remember to add new things to your gratitude list
    each day. This little practice helps shift your mind away
    from the "poor me syndrome" and helps you to truly be
    grateful for all the wonderful things in your life, even if
    they are just little things.

4. **Feed your mind with positive pictures, affirmations,
    books, audios**…Now this is very important, stay away
    from the news. Do not read the negative news in the
    newspaper (job want ads are ok, but nothing else!). Do not
    watch the news on TV or listen to news on the radio. All
    that negative crap does is fill your mind with doubts and
    fears and discouragement. Let all the other jobseekers
    listen to that crud. Let it affect them negatively, but don't
    let it affect you negatively. If you want to get a job fast
    you need to be an upbeat, positive thinking, happy, well-
    balanced, enjoyable person. And if you practice these four
    things as your daily ritual, plus use the great people skill
    techniques shown below, you'll have a great job in no time
    at all!

The 5 Simple People Skills That Will Help You Succeed More Than Anything Else!

I can't even begin to tell you how many ways these 5 people skills have improved my life. You have to experience them for yourself! I remember the first time I did these consciously every day for 7 days. I attracted so many beautiful people into my life and enjoyed deeper connections with others than I had ever experienced before! You've got to try these for yourself.

The following people skill techniques are adapted from Dale Carnegie's book, "How to Win Friends and Influence People", and Og Mandino's book, The Greatest Secret"! (both books are a must read if you want great people skills):

1.   Treat every person you speak with as "The Most Important Person In the World!"
2.   Smile sincerely at everyone you encounter (while silently in your mind saying "I Love You!").
3.   When talking with others, talk only about things that are of interest to the other person. Ask them questions about things they seem interested in and let them do most of the talking (be a good listener)!
4.   Remember and use people's first names throughout your conversations with them. A person's own name is a very sweet sound to them.
5.   Compliment people sincerely if there is something nice you can say about them.

When you practice these simple people skills consistently with everyone you meet as you job search, you'll find yourself winning more interviews and job offers automatically.

To Get Hired Faster – Remember What Companies Want

Who do hiring companies desperately look for? Bright, resourceful, talented, positive, committed people who have a pleasing personality and who get along well with others. That's who companies are looking for!

If you want a job fast you must communicate clearly in all of your job search documents (resume, cover letter, applications, thank you notes…), and especially in your interviews that you are… a bright, resourceful, talented, valuable, positive, committed individual with a pleasing personality and that you get along well with others.

Make it your personal mission to display and communicate these qualities throughout your job search. Be what companies want and need and I guarantee you'll land your next job much faster.

Physical Preparation

Now I have to admit I'm not the best at keeping up with physical exercise although I do eat a pretty good diet. So I'm not going to harp on this too much, but it is important. If you can stick with a simple exercise plan and eat a decent diet while you're searching for your new job, it will give you the following rewards…

1. It will help you deal with the stress of job searching effectively.
2. It will give you more energy and stamina to focus on your job search.
3. It will make you feel good about yourself and just make you physically feel good overall.

If at all possible try to eat healthy and do a little exercise. It'll just make the whole job search process nicer.

Document Preparation

Be sure to have all your job search documents ready.

You may not need all of the following documents, and some of them may not be appropriate for your type of work, but just make sure you have the types of documents you're going to need for your particular job search. Here's a list of documents you may want to have ready.

- Base resume
- Base cover letter
- Scannable / text based resume and cover letter
- Samples of your work:
    - Research you've conducted
    - Documents you've prepared
    - Publications you've written
- List of your accomplishments
- Reference letters and letters of recommendation
- Awards and honors:
- Conferences and workshops you've attended related to your work
- Certifications, college degrees and transcripts, training classes
- Other professional development:
    - Clubs, associations, conferences, if any self-study
- Community service participation
- Any other documents a potential employer would be interested in

The Most Effective Ways To Find Your Next Job

At this point, if you've followed all the directions in this book you should be well prepared to begin your job search. There are indeed a number of ways to look for a job, some are effective, some not so much. Here I thought I would share with you the most effective ways to search for a job.

Listed below are two different versions of statistics about effective job searches. First are The Top 5 Job Search Methods by Effectiveness (according to the United States Department of Labor):

1.   Contact companies directly (64.5% effective)
2.   Send out resumes and applications (48.3% effective)
3.   Public employment agencies (20.5% effective)
4.   Help wanted ads (14.5% effective)
5.   Friends, family, networking with contacts (13.5% effective)

Below is another group of statistics provided by another source from the 1980s…

1.   Research companies and contact decision makers through existing contacts (86% effective)
2.   Applying at companies without doing research (47% effective)
3.   Networking through friends and family to find job leads (34% effective)
4.   Getting help through a college/school placement office you have attended (21% effective)
5.   Ads in newspapers (the better the job, the less successful this method is) (5-24% effective)

What I find most interesting about these 2 different set of statistics is that between 1980 and today one thing has not changed in the job search world. Contacting companies directly (researching them and contacting decision makers directly) is consistently the most effective way and the quickest way to find a job.

Also interesting to me is that the vast majority of job seekers do not do this. When YOU DO, you'll find your next good job much faster!

Introducing Your Job-Getting Strategy

To maximize your chances of getting a job quickly, you'll want to go after your main job targets, your ideal "high end" types of jobs, "mid level" jobs you can do proficiently, and "low end" jobs you could do if you had to.

Here's a breakdown of what you need to do, and how much time you need to spend on each area to get that next job.

1. Find Companies With Posted Job Openings and Apply. Strive to make direct contact with hiring managers wherever you can. (spend 35% of your job search here). Here are a few places to look…
   a. Internet Job Postings (I'll show you the top sites for this shortly)
   b. Want ads in local papers and other publications
   c. Job boards
   d. Local job fairs.
2. Find Companies With No-Posted Job Openings and Make Direct Contact with them (Yes, call them on the phone) (spend 35% of your job search here). Here are a few places to look…

a. Local Business Search Tools (I'll show you a few in a moment)
b. Phone Books and Local Directories
c. Local Papers and Other Publications

3. Network with Friends, Family, and Local Job Support Groups 15% of your time. You may want to use some online tools such as Linked-In and Twitter to network with others as well. Just remember to be professional at all times no matter what method you use so nothing comes back to bite you later.

4. Follow up better than everyone else 15% of your time.
a. Follow up on resume's you've sent.
b. Follow up with contacts you've made at companies.
c. Follow up with thank you letters to interviewers and others.

Where To Begin Your Job Search – Top 10 Job Search Sites

Start searching for job openings and opportunities with Companies who have Posted Job Openings. Use these Top 10 Recommended Job Search Sites…

Simply go to each site and use their free job search services. Look for job openings by job type and location, post your resume on sites that provide that service, apply for any openings that match your skills and interests, network with others. Remember to search and apply for all your top job targets. Use whatever you can find on these sites that will help you find your next great job.

1. www.monster.com
2. www.indeed.com
3. www.usa.gov

4. www.careerbuilder.com
5. www.dice.com
6. www.linkup.com
7. www.simplyhired.com
8. www.linkedin.com
9. www.craigslist.com

Another resource that can be extremely helpful in researching different types of jobs, their salary ranges, projected growth in the next few years is provided by the U.S. Department of Labor. You can check it out at the following link.

10. http://www.bls.gov/ooh/

The Most Effective Way To Use LinkedIn

Although all of the sites listed above are helpful to a degree, (#9) LinkedIn is quickly becoming one of the most powerful tools for finding a job.

Some companies are actually searching for job candidates on LinkedIn. Recruiters also use LinkedIn to search for potential candidates. Companies and recruiters can easily search here for candidates in their industry, find work history information, recommendations, references, and other helpful information.

Job searchers can look for jobs on LinkedIn using keywords, location, or by using the "Advanced Search" features to get even more specific.

If you don't have a LinkedIn profile now is the time to start one. If you already have one, make sure you maximize your profile. Here are some great tips to help you make the most of this tool…

- Create a detailed LinkedIn profile that includes all of your vital information, your job history, your industry, education…
- Ask coworkers and former bosses to recommend you on LinkedIn.
- List your skills and the same keywords you use in your resume throughout your profile.
- Post your photo. You can post a small professional (face shot) photo up to 80x80 pixels to your profile.
- Use the "Answers" feature to respond to questions and to ask for additional information.
- Connect with other members and invite them to be part of your network. Search for people in your industry to connect with and send them an invite to join your network.
- Take advantage of LinkedIn Mobile so you can stay connected from anywhere from your phone.

Once you complete your LinkedIn profile you can do the following to help you find a job…

- Use the search tool to look for companies who are hiring.
- Ask for more recommendations from colleagues to make your profile more attractive to companies and recruiters.
- Grow your network by sending invites out to as many people as you can find in your industry. Simply use the invite feature and send a brief note letting them know that you want to network with people in your industry so that you can potentially be a great resource for each other.
- Notify your network that you are interested in new career opportunities (be careful not to notify people from your current job though if you don't want them to know :-)

- Locate hiring managers at companies. Reach out to friends in your network (ones you have built a relationship with) and find out who the hiring manager is at their company for the type of position you are after.
- Use the advanced search feature to look for new startup companies who may need your expertise. Just search on the word "startup" and include the industry you like in the company or keyword fields.
- Start building your network right now and continue throughout your career. It's better to have a huge network before you need it!

Of all the online job search sites available, LinkedIn is a must for most professionals.

Where To Find Local Employers and Businesses That Need You

Listed below are a couple of local business search sites. Here you can search for businesses in your area that would employ people with your skill set. For example, search on electronics, retail, warehouse, restaurant, architect, accounting, grocer, food supply, trucking… Whatever types of businesses would need your skills.

Find local companies using the following search tools. When you find potential employers, get their phone number and call them. Ask for the manager of the department you would work for (accounting, telecom, administrative…).

Once you have the manager, introduce yourself and briefly (30 seconds or less) tell them about your experience, training, skills, express your value to them, and ask them what types of opportunities they have for someone with your background!

If they don't have any at this time, ask if it would be ok to check back with them in a few weeks or a month. Also ask them if they are aware of any other managers or companies who could use your skills! Then track your conversation and note when you are to call back!

Local Search Links For Businesses:
http://www.thinklocal.com/
http://www.indeed.com

Other methods for finding local jobs...

- Search online for local job boards or job banks in your area.
- Check with your local Chamber of Commerce.
- Local Yellow Pages (online).
- Attend local job fairs.
- Look in local papers and Business Journals for Job Want Ads and Potential Businesses to contact.
- Contact former employers in good standing.
- Network with friends and co-workers (and or former co-workers).

Other Job Search Sites (A List of 50 Top Job Search Sites)

Quintcareers.com is another fantastic resource for helping job hunters. The only problem is a person can get lost on their site because they have so much great information.

I suggest you simply go to the link below to check out their list of Top 50 Job Search Sites, do this only after you've used the Top 10 Job Search Sites listed above in this document. Then you can check out these additional 50 resources if you've fully utilized the original Top 10 list. Just don't overload yourself and lose focus on your job search. These sites are all meant to be tools, not distractions ☺

Here's Quintcareers.com Top 50 Recommended Job Search Sites:

http://www.quintcareers.com/top_50_sites.html

Create a List of Companies to Contact and Keep Adding To It

Find as many companies as you can using the methods outlined in this chapter, then start contacting them one by one and track every call you make.

Tracking and Follow Up For A Good Job Now and A Better One Later

As you begin to send out resumes and build new contacts at companies, you'll need to track everything you're doing. This is where you gain a real advantage over the majority of people who never take this step. It will not only help you in your current job search, but if you decide to change jobs in the future, some of your new found contacts may prove to be super valuable!

Resume Tracking List Example: Here is a basic tracking form you can use to track the resumes you've sent out so you can follow up…

Date Sent	Company	Contact Info	Notes	Next Follow up Date

Top Success Secrets for Finding Hidden Job Openings

It's well known that a very large percentage of available jobs are not even advertised anywhere. And the only way to find these hidden jobs is to prospect for opportunities by directly contacting companies.

Now I realize for many of you that does not sound appealing at all. And I can understand that, but the fact remains this is one of the best ways to find a good job quickly, without a lot of competition.

I know from personal experience that this works quite well. When I was laid off and needed to find a job quickly, I started calling companies directly and asking for the hiring managers of a department I would be able to work in.

I would let the hiring manager know that I was interested in finding work in this field and asked them for their advice and expertise on the best way to go about that. I also asked them if they knew of any job openings and asked if I could call them back in a month to check on any opportunities.

After only a few weeks of calling around (and I didn't even put in as many hours as I should have), I found a manager that was at least willing to have me come in for an interview. I went in for the interview and was offered the job that day. The hiring manager was particularly impressed that I had called around and asked for advice and was actively seeking opportunity. He thought it showed initiative. All I know is, I found a job, fast!

This same principle certainly applies today. As I noted earlier the United States Department of Labor listed this method (contacting companies directly) as the top method for finding a job.

I think you understand the importance of making yourself do this. So here is the best advice and coaching I can give you for contacting companies directly. Actually, here's a strategy that will help you maximize this powerful job search method.

#1. Build Your Confidence Before You Start

- Review your resume and the self assessment you did in the second chapter of this book before you start your job search each day, and especially right before you contact a company directly. This will help you remember just how great you really are, and help you remember what you have to offer prospective employers.
- Visualize yourself being at your best on each call. Imagine yourself being charming, witty, smart, and likable. Imagine you and the hiring manager having a great conversation together, with them being very impressed with you.
- Write out a short script of what you are going to say when you speak to the hiring manager. Rehearse it, practice it in front of the mirror until you speak it with confidence in a clear, comfortable, likable voice. Keep in mind you don't have to repeat this script word for word when you call a potential

employer, that would be a little unnatural. Just use this little exercise to keep you prepared so you know what to say when the time comes.

#2 Look at It As a Game and <u>Don't</u> Take Rejection Personally.

- Sure, a number of people will not want to talk to you. Some of them may even be rude. But don't take it personal, they don't even know you. They're just busy people trying to avoid interruptions. If a manager does not want to talk to you, it has nothing to do with you. Just look at it for what it is, nothing. And keep calling. The more you do this the sooner you'll have that job. ☺

#3 Research The Company's History, Needs, Goals and Mission Before Calling

- Try to look up company information on the web before you contact any business and get an idea of their mission, their products, their services, their goals, and so on. So you're better prepared to talk with them about their needs.

#4 Always Ask to Speak to the Hiring Manager for the Position You're After.

- When you call the front desk of any company, ask to speak to the manager of the department you want to work in. When you get through to a manager, greet them nicely, thank them for taking your call, and give them a quick 30 second pitch about what you do well, how you can benefit them, and how you are very interested in opportunities with their company! Then ask if you can send a resume or if you can meet with them in person. If the front desk won't put you through to the hiring manager, ask if you can leave a message. Then just leave your name and number for them to call you back. If they ask what it's for, just let them know you're interested in working for their department.

#5 Take Notes and Follow up
- As you have a conversation with any hiring manager be sure to take good notes and ask when you can call them back. Note the date and time to call them back, then make sure that you do.

The primary goal of a cold call for a job is to get an appropriate hiring manager on the phone and to get them to agree to meet with you at their office.

Guaranteed Step-By-Step Job Finding Tactics

Ok, now you know that the best way to find a job quickly is by directly contacting companies (yes via the telephone). And the best approach for landing an interview via direct contact is to show that you are a person who can add incredible value. Show that you are the ideal person to help solve their hiring need.

Although every call you make will be unique (and you need to remain flexible in your conversation), you want to cover the following main objectives during your initial call…

1. Introduce yourself: Introduce yourself with a little zeal, have life in your voice, use a little enthusiasm **EXAMPLE**; *"Hi, this is Tom Jones."*

2. In less than 30 seconds explain your work background and your experience level, **EXAMPLE**; *"I'm an auto mechanic with 7 years of extensive experience and I'm calling to find out what your hiring requirements are for someone with my background."* (Use your own job skills and experience of course, but I think you get the idea of what to say, based on this example).

Next let them know some of the top skills that set you apart from other applicants, **EXAMPLE**; *"I am a certified mechanic on Toyota, GM, and Ford automobiles and in my most recent position I was considered the top transmission specialist in our crew."* (Talk about your particular strengths and value).

Tell them you are very interested in their company, and ask if they would be willing to tell you a little about his or her department, their current needs, and about any potential opportunities they may have, now or in the future.

3. Ask to meet them for an interview: Then just ask, **EXAMPLE**; *"When would be a good time for me to stop by so we can meet in person"*. Or say something like, *"I would be glad to drop off my resume so we can meet in person, when is a good time for you?"*

Do your best to contact the hiring manager directly. Keep in mind that a number of them will try to avoid you because they are busy. If they won't have a conversation with you, simply ask if you can send them your resume and cover letter and ask if you can contact them at a future time to follow up.

Don't let rejection bother you, it's not personal. This is just a numbers game. The more hiring managers you contact the sooner you'll find someone who's hiring and the sooner you'll find a job. That's it, it's just a numbers game. Besides if you run into a few rude people (some hiring managers) over the phone, there's a good chance you wouldn't want to work for them anyway. So just keep calling. Keep calling until you find the right job for you.

Stick with it, be diligent, this is the key to your job search success.

What If You Get Their Voice Mail?

If you call 10 hiring managers, you may be lucky to reach 3 or 4 of them live on the phone. There's a very good chance you'll get the hiring manager's voice mailbox a lot of the time.

So what should you do if you get a hiring manager's voicemail? I think it's a good practice to leave a brief message with callback information. Just make sure your message is scripted and practiced so it sounds solid when they listen to it. Here's an example of what you're scripted message may be like…

"Hi, this is Tom Jones. I'm an auto mechanic with 7 years of extensive hands-on experience and I'm calling to find out what your hiring requirements are for someone with my background. I am a certified mechanic on Toyota, GM, and Ford automobiles, and am considered by my peers to be the top transmission specialist in our crew.

I am very interested in learning more about your company's needs, and in how I may be able to benefit your organization. Please give me a call back at 555-123-4567 at your earliest convenience. Again my name is Tom Jones and my call back number is 555-123-4567. Thank you for your time and I hope the rest of your day goes well!

That's it. Simply introduce yourself, tell them your qualifications including your top skills and your value, let them know you're interested and leave your callback information.

Direct Calling Success Tips

Here are a few additional tips that will help you be more successful as you do direct calling as part of your job search.

1. Timing: the best time for direct calling is early in the day between 7:30 a.m. and 9:30 a.m. and later in the day between 3 p.m. and 5 p.m. another thing to remember is that the person you are calling could be busy, or distracted with other things. If you sense that they are distracted or too busy, always ask if there's a better time for you to call back. Then call them back at the time they recommend.

2. Do a little research on each company you're going to contact, before you call them. You can usually find out quite a bit from the Web, or you can get hints from their Yellow Page ads. It's just a good idea for you to be prepared with a little knowledge about the company you are talking to before you contact them.

3. IMPORTANT: Don't begin your call by asking them if there are any job openings. You are not asking for job. You are proposing to benefit their team or organization with your skills, experience and abilities (your unique value).

4. Always strive to directly contact the hiring manager of the department you would work for. You can get their number by contacting the front desk and asking for the manager of the department you are interested in. If they ask who you are and why you are calling, just tell them you are researching companies who operate this type of department and you just want to ask the manager of that department a few quick questions, or just tell them you are interested in learning about opportunities in that department. You may only get through 50%, maybe less, but that's okay. This is just a numbers game. If you don't get through the first time continue to contact other companies until you get through. Make notes and call this company back at a later time. It may take you three or more tries to get through. The more hiring managers you contact the sooner you'll get a job.

The Go Getters Get The Jobs!

Company's like to hire go-getters, people who show initiative! If you put forth the time focus and effort into finding your next job, you'll find a job much faster than 95% of all other job searchers!

If you apply the same focus, effort, and commitment to your new job (once you land it), you'll probably find you're one of the best workers in the place. As we've said, the best workers with the best attitude almost always make more money, have better job security, and enjoy more job satisfaction overall.

Be excellent in all you do! Do your best, give your all and you will be successful in your job search, and in your career.

All you need now is to master the art of interviewing!

CHAPTER 5 – Powerful Job-Winning Interview Tactics

It's funny to me now, but I used to hate the whole interview process! I used to be focused on all the wrong things, things that were out of my control. Once I started focusing on all the things I could control my interviews got a lot easier, and a lot better!

Confidence, people skills, positive mindset, the ability to communicate well, and being very prepared, these five things will enable you to ace almost any interview you do. And that's exactly what this chapter is all about.

You can acquire all five of these required interview-acing-skills by simply practicing the things you learn in this chapter. First, read this entire chapter to learn everything you can about excellent interviewing skills. Then practice the interviewing skills you learn here in front of a mirror.

Practice reading through the interview questions and answering them out loud in front of a mirror. Use the mirror so you can observe and improve your body language and your facial expressions. Practice standing and sitting with confidence and using friendly confident facial expressions. Practice the positive mindset skills you learned in the first chapter of this book. Practice the five simple people skills outlined, that will help win over your interviewer.

Review your talents, skills, abilities, and accomplishments from the second chapter, and practice talking about them in front of a mirror. Practice everything you learn in this chapter (and from other chapters in this book), until you feel confident in your ability to do well in an interview!

I'll show you everything you need to know to perform a super successful interview so you can get more job offers!

Let's get started…

Top Tips for Successful Interviewing

Know Thyself

Confidence is an important personal trait to have. It's even more important when you get to the interview stage.

The quickest and easiest way to build your own confidence before an interview is to go back and read through the self-assessment, career assessments, personality profiles, skills and accomplishments that you documented in the second chapter of this book.

It's always good to remind yourself of just how great you are and just how many talents and abilities you have. It really helps a lot to do this before any interview.

It will dramatically increase your confidence in yourself and your abilities, and it will help you prepare to communicate your value to the prospective employer.

Review your skills and assessments before any interview to help you remember your true value and to help you communicate that value in the best possible way.

Plan the Outcome In Advance

If you want something to turn out a certain way you'll need to have an outcome in mind. This principle is practiced by almost all super successful people, it's also practiced by successful businesses, lovers, artists, sports stars… you name it.

Successful businesses decide what they want their business to accomplish and they create plans to make it happen. Tthey have a specific outcome in mind. Many professional sports stars use visualization before a game to help them focus on the outcome they want. Professional speakers visualize themselves giving their speeches in advance in order to affect their desired outcome.

We will use this same principle to help you prepare for the outcome you want when you interview for a job.

Let's break this down in terms of an interview.

If I were getting ready for a job interview here are the things I would want to define for the outcome of that interview:

1. I want to be perceived as the top candidate.
2. I want the interviewer to really personally like me and to be impressed with what I can do for them.
3. I want to feel confident and come across as very personable and enjoyable.
4. I want to feel calm and comfortable.

5. I want the interviewer to genuinely feel comfortable with me and I want both the interviewer and myself to be in sync, (to feel a friendly connection and mutual respect for one another).
6. I want to nail every interview question with the best possible answer I could give to this specific interviewer.
7. I want to look and feel my best.
8. I want to feel upbeat, energetic, and enthusiastic.
9. I want to communicate everything in the most effective and positive way.
10. When the interview is over I want the interviewer to decide in their mind that they must absolutely hire me for the position. I want them to desperately want me for the job.

Hopefully these 10 items will give you a few ideas of how to decide the outcome of your own interview.

Go ahead and write out the outcomes you desire for your next interview. Go wild with it, don't hold back! Once you've defined the outcome you desire, visualize yourself conducting the best possible interview in all your regal glory, being at your best and impressing your interviewer so much that they simply can't wait to hire you.

Visualize this scene before going to sleep and upon waking each day for several days before your interview! The results can be pretty amazing!

Remember To Use These 5 Simple People Skills During All of Your Interviews!

Remember to use the five simple people skills you learned in the last chapter whenever you have an interview. Here they are again to refresh your memory:

- Treat every person you speak with as "The Most Important Person in the World!"

- Smile sincerely at everyone you encounter (while silently in your mind saying "I Love You!").

- When talking with others, talk only about things that are of interest to the other person. Ask them questions about things they seem interested in and let them do most of the talking (be a good listener)!

- Remember and use people's names throughout your conversations with them (ie..Cindy that is awesome!).

- Compliment people sincerely if there is something nice you can say about them.

The Art of Mental Preparation

To insure you have a job winning mindset for your interview, go back to the first section of this e-book titled "Creating Your Job Winning Mindset". Review that chapter and apply the skills you learned there.

Hopefully you've been practicing many of the techniques outlined in that section. In any case, just go back to review the techniques that will put you in the best possible mindset for your interview.

If you've done the techniques suggested when you first read the "Creating Your Job Winning Mindset" section, you'll know they don't take very long at all to do. More importantly they really do work incredibly well! Those techniques will give you a very positive, confident, job winning mindset that will help you come across as a top candidate when you interview.

Research the Potential Employer

This is important. A common complaint I and many other hiring managers have, is that so many job candidates have not even researched our companies before we interview them. By far the most impressive candidates always do some research about a company before they interview. The more they know about the hiring company they are interviewing with the more impressive they are.

Here are some great tips for researching companies before your interview:

1. Call the company on the phone and requests sales literature, product brochures, annual reports, and any other type of information that will help you understand what the company does.

2. Go to the company's web site and make notes about what the company sells, what their advantages are, what their goals and values are. If they have a press release section on their web site, read through their press releases to see what they have been doing lately. Read any section that has a company profile or "About Us" information. Look for any job profile or job posting information that will give you more details about the position you are applying for.

3. Do a Google search on the company name and look for any information published about the company you'll be interviewing with.

4. Look for any information you can find about their competition. Visit their competitions web sites to understand how they market themselves. Your interviewers will be impressed that you understand their business.

5. Finally, prepare a list of the products and services the hiring company offers. Be sure to understand their customers, and how your skills can fit in and benefit their company.

Common Interview Questions to Prepare For

Here are a few of the most common interview questions you'll hear during an interview and some good suggestions on how to answer them.

1. Tell me about yourself? Keep your answer under two minutes and only talk about things that pertain to your ability to do the job you are interviewing for.

2. What are your greatest strengths? Be prepared to talk about what you do well and how you can use those strengths in this position to benefit the company.

3. What are your greatest weaknesses? Don't say things like, "I'm a workaholic" or "I'm a perfectionist" as these are overused statements. You may just want to say something like… "I know that nobody's perfect but I really don't get complaints about my work. I just prefer to focus on doing my best, improving myself and my skills, and on adding value. I

figure if I focus on these I shouldn't have too many weaknesses!

4. What do you know about our company? If you've followed the directions we gave above and did a good job of researching the company, you will be well prepared to answer this question.

5. If you took this job what could you accomplish in the first year? Gear your answer toward how quickly you can learn and on how you hope to improve things for them by applying your talents, abilities, knowledge and skills.

Great links to Common Interview Questions and The Best Ways to Answer Them

Go to the sites listed below, read through the questions and answers and practice answering them in front of a mirror. This exercise will give you great confidence in answering almost any question you will face during an interview.

http://www.best-interview-strategies.com/questions.html

http://www.quintcareers.com/interview_question_database/interview_questions_1.html

http://www.bspcn.com/2007/08/24/10-killer-job-interview-questions-and-answers/

25 Difficult Interview Questions and How To Answer Them

The following link is to an excellent reprinted article from FOCUS Magazine. It does a very nice job of outlining 25 of the most common/difficult questions you may be asked in an interview, and provides advice on how to handle them. Make sure you check this article out before your next interview!

http://www.datsi.fi.upm.es/~frosal/docs/25mdq.html

NOTE: Some of the questions may not apply to the position you are seeking, but many of these will apply. Just review and practice answering the questions that could apply to you.

Impressive Questions You Must Ask Your Interviewer To Make The Absolute Best Impression

Another thing that will absolutely impress your interviewer is if you ask excellent questions! Always ask questions in a respectful way and in a positive way (you don't want to give the impression that you're trying to find fault). Here are some great questions you may want to ask your interviewer after they're finished asking you questions…

1. What are the most important objectives you'd like to see accomplished in this position over the next 3, 6, and 12 months?

2. What do you feel are the greatest challenges I would face if I accept this position?

3. What are your thoughts on how these challenges could best be handled?

4. Why is this position currently open?

5. What type of support does this position receive in terms of finances, people, and other resources?

6. What sort of freedom would be allowed in determining my own work objectives, deadlines, and productivity measurements?

7. What type of events and opportunities are there for successful, progressive employees?

8. How will the person in this position be evaluated for performance?

9. What do you feel are the greatest keys to being successful in this position?

10. What significant changes do you foresee for this position and for this company in the near future?

Asking great questions will show your interviewer that you take this job opportunity seriously and that you think things through! This will always impress an interviewer.

The Top 10 Interview Mistakes People Make and How to Avoid Them

There are a number of common mistakes people make when interviewing and you need to be certain you avoid them. Below is a list of common mistakes people make.

1. **Showing up too late or too early**: This generally leaves a bad impression with an interviewer as they are very busy and have scheduled this valuable time with you. The best practice is to show up about five minutes before the interview unless otherwise requested.

2. **Inappropriate dress**: We are all judged by our appearance (whether we like it or not). It may not be fair. It may not be right. But the fact is people are human beings with biases and they will knowingly or unknowingly judge us on how we appear to them. Just like we may unknowingly judge others on how they appear to us. Whatever job you're applying for, make sure you dress in your best clothes that are acceptable for that position. Make sure your clothes are clean and pressed so you look your best. I can't tell you how many times I've seen people come in wearing wrinkled or dirty clothes or inappropriate clothing for the position they are interviewing for. It's not the single determining factor of whether a person gets the job or not, but I'll guarantee you it weighs into the choice of who gets a job or not.

3. **Poor handshake**: Believe it or not a handshake leaves an impression with an interviewer. Your handshake should not be too limp or too strong. When you shake hands your hand shake should be firm. And as you shake hands, smile a sincere smile, look into the interviewer's eyes, and silently in your mind and

in your heart say, "I am really glad to meet you!" that will
leave the best impression.

4. **Being unprepared**: So many people are unprepared when they
    come to an interview. They don't seem to know anything
    about the company. They are unprepared to answer many
    common interview questions, and they don't ask any questions
    of the interviewer. As we've talked about in this entire
    section, be prepared. Know your strengths and your value and
    be ready to communicate it. Research the company and know
    as much as you can about them. Be prepared to answer
    common interview questions. Be prepared to ask excellent
    questions of the interviewer. Ask about the company and the
    position. Be prepared to be at your best because you only get
    one shot at each interview.

5. **Poor communication skills and poor interview etiquette**:
    Some people come to interviews with very poor
    communication skills and poor etiquette. Every hiring manager
    has stories to tell about this. The bottom line is, turn off your
    cell phone, don't bring food or drink into an interview, don't
    ever be rude, always be professional. Try not to talk too much
    and only talk about things that pertain to your ability to do the
    job you are interviewing for. Make sure you talk enough about
    your value, your passion for this type of work, and your desire
    to come and work for them. Always be courteous, don't
    interrupt, smile and be polite. You also want to make good eye
    contact with the interviewer throughout the process. Practice
    answering interview questions in front of a mirror. This will
    help you to communicate more clearly and help you to be
    aware of your facial expressions and your body language.
    Insure your communication is effective and confident.

6. **Badmouthing previous employers or coworkers**: People who come to interviews and badmouth previous employers or coworkers are perceived as very negative. Whatever you do, don't say anything negative about a previous boss, a previous employer, or any previous people you've worked with. Even if you have plenty of ammo and it's all true do not do it. Employers want positive balanced people who get along well with others. And besides your interviewer may be good friends with someone you badmouth.

7. **Lying**: Just don't do it! If you get caught lying on your resume or in your interview you will automatically be ruled out for the job.

8. **Complaining**: I don't know anyone who likes a complainer, and I don't know any hiring managers who've hired a person who complains incessantly during an interview.

9. **Being too nervous**: Although it's normal to be a little nervous during an interview, too much nervousness can be a bad thing. Nervousness can be misinterpreted. Be sure to take deep breaths, do some exercise before you go to an interview, anything that will help you to relax. If you follow the directions in this book, you should be very well-prepared for the interview and that in itself should help you be more confident and less nervous.

10. **Being too confident**: Being too confident or too cocky can also hurt you in an interview. In the same way no one likes a complainer, no one likes a pompous know it all. If you have a strong personality and you're trying to impress an interviewer, the best thing you can do is employ a little humility. Show your value, show your strengths, and be confident about who you are, but also show that you value others. Demonstrate that

you can work well with others and get along with others. If you show your value in a respectful sincere way, you'll go a lot farther with the interviewer.

Interview Preparations Summary Tips

Here's a quick summary of steps you should take to prepare yourself to do the best interviews possible!

1. Create a positive upbeat mindset by using the skills you learned in the first chapter of this book.

2. Build your personal charisma by practicing the top people skills techniques referenced in this chapter and outlined in the last chapter.

3. Review your talents, skills, abilities, and accomplishments and practice talking about them in front of a mirror, into a video camera, or to a friend.

4. Determine the desired outcome for your interview and visualize it intensely using all 5 of your senses. Imagine the outcome as being real in your mind.

5. Practice answering interview questions in the best possible way in front of a mirror, a video camera, or in front of a friend.

6. Practice asking your outstanding questions to the interviewer!

7. Visualize your desired outcome (for several days before an interview) in great detail, using all 5 senses in your imagination.

Have fun with it! Be relaxed and look at it as a game. A game you intend to win!

Practice, Practice, Practice… Then go to your interview, do your best, and trust completely that it will work out if it is supposed to, and that it won't if it's not! If a job doesn't work out, trust that there's an even better opportunity on the way.

You Now Have Everything You Need To Land A Job Fast

Focus on keeping your Job-Winning-Mindset, prepare your interview-getting- resume, keep searching for job opportunities, practice interviewing and be prepared…over and over till you've got that great new job!

One thing is for sure, there's a great job coming your way very soon. If you practice what you've learned in this book!

Additional Resources to Help You Get Your Next Job Faster…

Visit www.markduin.com for additional resources that will help you get the results you want!

About The Author

Mark Duin is a former drug addict 9th grade dropout, now part of the management team for a multimillion dollar technology business.

An internationally recognized author and award winning speaker, Mark inspires and instructs people on how to experience an extraordinary life of success, happiness, personal fulfillment, and contribution.

He is a recognized expert on overcoming challenges and on maximizing human potential. Mark combines spiritual principles, success principles, accelerated learning and advanced personal development methods to enable people to live an incredibly exciting and rewarding life!

Talented, inspirational, warm, funny and profound, Mark is a motivational speaker who addresses a variety of topics relating to business, career, and personal success.

Meet Mark at www.markduin.com and get valuable free training that will help you enjoy an extraordinary life of prosperity passion and purpose!